W9-DGD-929

MY
LADYE NEVELLS
BOOKE

MY LADYE NEVELLS BOOKE

OF VIRGINAL MUSIC

BY

WILLIAM BYRD

Edited, with Historical and Analytical Notes, by
HILDA ANDREWS, Mus.Bac.

Preface by
SIR RICHARD TERRY

WITH A NEW INTRODUCTION BY

BLANCHE WINOGRON

Mannes College of Music, New York City

Dover Publications, Inc., New York

This Dover edition, first published in 1969, is an unabridged and unaltered republication of the work originally published by J. Curwen & Sons Ltd., London, in 1926. A new Introduction has been written specially for the present edition by Blanche Winogron.

Standard Book Number: 486-22246-2
Library of Congress Catalog Card Number: 68-55532

Manufactured in the United States of America

DOVER PUBLICATIONS, INC.
180 Varick Street
New York, N. Y. 10014

DEDICATED

BY PERMISSION

TO THE

LADY HENRY NEVILL

INTRODUCTION TO THE DOVER EDITION

A bird I have that sings so well,
  None like to her their tunes can raise;
All other birds she doth excel,
  And of birds all best worthy praise.

Now this my bird of endless fame,
  Whose music sweet, whose pleasant sound,
Whose worthy praise, whose worthy name,
  Doth from the earth to heaven rebound.

THIS anonymous contemporary song text reflects the love and reverence for William Byrd felt by his peers and by those whom he served so well. His genius won for him a unique place in the musical world of Tudor England. From 1569 on, he held the honored and powerful position of Gentleman of the Chapel Royal. Moreover, in this time of religious turbulence, Byrd, a seemingly sedate man and a great favorite of the Queen, was one of the Catholics never seriously threatened.[1] To our knowledge he had never been involved in a plot against Elizabeth, her Church or her government. She called him "a stiff Papist and a good subject." She had audible proof of his absolute dedication to his art above all else, for his musical activities were in all forms, and transcended religious boundaries: either because of a personal philosophy, or because, astutely, he wrote for both the Catholic Church and the prevailing Anglican Church. He himself considered this corpus of sacred music, and the choral music as a whole, his greatest work. However, the keyboard music, which includes many gems, blazed trails for his contemporaries and all who followed in the centuries to come. *The Fitzwilliam Virginal Book* and the Nevill commonplace book, *My Ladye Nevells Booke,* are our two chief sources for this music.

Music printing was slow getting started in England; in fact, England was fifty years behind the Continent in this respect.[2] The few books which had been printed were pro-

[1] Many compositions by Byrd figured among the several hundred sheaves of virginal music which some of his suspect recusant colleagues smuggled into the prison quarters of the elder and then the younger Francis Tregian. The chief manuscript compilation of these compositions, which has preserved for us the greater part of the English virginal school, is now known as the *Fitzwilliam Virginal Book.* See Sydney Beck's notes to Dover Recording HCR-5226 (HCR-ST-7015), *A Program of Selections from the Fitzwilliam Virginal Book,* pp. 1–3.

[2] Byrd's career is also connected with the history of music printing in England. He and Thomas Tallis, allegedly his teacher, held the royal patent for the printing of music books and paper beginning in 1575. After the death of Tallis in 1585, Byrd alone held the patent until 1596.

hibitively expensive. Players had for a long time been accustomed to copying out what pleased them, creating personal and family "commonplace books." Several of the manuscript virginal books which have come to light were commonplace books; many other such collections must have disappeared in the almost 400 years' span of time.

In 1591, when the Nevill commonplace book was presented to the Lady Nevill then living, instrumental music had already developed to a remarkable degree, but vocal music was at its height, artistically and as a popular pastime. Perhaps for this reason alone, immediately after the English victory over the Spanish Armada in 1588, with the country in a mood of glorious jubilation, the people more affluent and the political climate somewhat more relaxed, Byrd had gathered together the accumulation of some years' work and published his *Psalmes, Sonets and songs of Sadnes and pietie.* In 1589 he published the *Songs of sundrie natures* and the first book of his *Cantiones sacrae.* During these years he was living in Harlington, between Eridge Castle in Sussex, the seat of the Nevill family, whom he knew and may have served as music instructor, and Windsor, the home of his friend John Baldwin, the most famous musical scribe of the time. Probably Byrd corrected the manuscript many times while the volume, obviously commissioned by some member of the Nevill family, was being compiled.

Why did Byrd not publish these pieces too? For one thing, we know that he himself most prized his sacred choral and vocal music, especially when it was inspired by "the life of the words."[3] Then, perhaps his integrity did not permit him to do for himself what he could not with impunity do for his suspect friends, colleagues and co-religionists. Perhaps, also, the demand for keyboard music did not yet justify the great expense involved. And perhaps, as Edmund Fellowes has suggested in his definitive biography of Byrd, the physical problems of printing the ornate keyboard variations had not yet been solved. This seems questionable, for as early as 1599 Byrd's successor in the printing monopoly, Thomas Morley, brought out his *First Booke of Consort Lessons* with a printed lute part. We know now that the elaborate writing for the lute, direct antecedent and greatest influence upon the keyboard literature, was in its own way a printing problem. Since this 1599 lute part book is still lost we cannot compare Morley's solution[4] with the first printed book of virginal music, *Parthenia,* devoted to pieces by William Byrd, John Bull and Orlando Gibbons, which did not appear until 1611 or 1612. Significantly, by that time the Catholic James I was on the throne, the political picture had changed and it was safer for the three colleagues to be openly associated in one publication. Back in 1599 Morley, too, may have been protecting some of the recusant composers whose music was included in his collection

[3] E. H. Fellowes, *William Byrd,* Oxford University Press, London, 1936, p. 235.

[4] *The First Booke of Consort Lessons,* Collected by Thomas Morley, Reconstructed and Edited with an Introduction and Critical Notes by Sydney Beck, C. F. Peters Corporation, for The New York Public Library, New York, 1959, p. 37.

by leaving them anonymous, a fact for which he was criticized in 1614 by Rosseter in the latter's similar volume, and is still criticized now.[5]

In 1968 the identity of "Lady Nevill" remains as mysterious as it was in 1926 when the first edition of the present volume appeared. In 1936 Edmund Fellowes, too, admitted the impossibility of a specific identification.[6] The genealogical lines and interrelationships of this old and distinguished Catholic family, which for centuries has supplied England with loyal servants on many levels, even to its highest administrators, are most complex. That the scribe John Baldwin signed and dated the completed manuscript in 1591 does not necessarily mean that the pieces included were commissioned or even written between 1588 and 1591 for the spirited, educated Lady Rachel, wife of the younger Sir Edward Nevill, Earl of Abergavenny and Member of Parliament from Windsor from 1588 to 1589. Like Byrd's 1588 *Psalmes . . .* and several of the elaborate broken consort settings that Morley compiled, some dating back to about 1575,[7] these compositions may represent the accumulation of ten to fifteen years' work. Lady Rachel probably inherited the volume, and treasuring it as a family heirloom—the manuscript is still in the hands of the present Abergavennys—would not change the monogram H. N. The latter, now in the lower left-hand corner of the title page and said to be not so old as the manuscript, may have been put there when the original binding, which customarily bore the owner's initials, had deteriorated and the volume was rebound. It seems more likely that the commonplace book was first commissioned by one of the three Henry Nevills, in particular the sixth Earl, whose wife Frances, also lively and literary, was mentioned in Horace Walpole's *A Catalogue of the Royal and Noble Authors of England* (1758). She died in 1576.

As should be expected, the character and musical tastes of both ladies, and perhaps of the whole family, seem to be reflected in the choice of pieces. Apart from the obviously programmed suite *The Battell* (supposedly written after the Armada victory), most of the themes are somber, academically treated at length. Of contemporary dances only the stately *Munsers Almaine* (*Monsieurs Almaine*) and the ten grave pavans with their rather subdued galliards are to be found, along with variations on only a few of the oldest traditional and country dance-tunes. Byrd elsewhere set many that were more varied in character. The scope of the volume, due to the omission of the delightful *corantos* and *voltas* so popular at court, is somewhat restricted. Were the Ladies Nevill, as members of an "attainted" family,[8] not welcomed at court? Did they dislike the less restrained Italian dances? Or did Byrd write these livelier pieces at a later time? They are included in the Fitzwilliam col-

[5] Morley, *op. cit.*, p. 4.

[6] *Ibid.*, p. 17.

[7] *Ibid.*, pp. 15, 16, 18, 19.

[8] Earlier members of the family had been involved in plots to overthrow the regime, and had lost their ancestral estates.

lection along with many other settings by Byrd of sacred and secular songs and popular tunes. At any rate, in view of the acute appreciation by Hilda Andrews of the character, variety, quality and importance of the virginal school as a whole, it is difficult to understand why she dismisses Byrd's contribution to the Fitzwilliam collection as unrepresentative, at the same time proclaiming the "splendid vitality of his inventive faculty, never surpassed and rarely equalled by any of his contemporaries"; or why in looking back to the beginnings of keyboard style and Hugh Aston's delightful *Hornepype* (*c.* 1500?) she should have missed the humor, the daring, and found it only "crude" and "tedious." It is true that today, with the old lacuna between Aston and Byrd almost filled by newly discovered manuscripts, we have a better perspective.[9]

The development of Byrd's keyboard style can be clearly traced to maturity in *My Ladye Nevells Booke.* The earlier pieces are still choral-bound; the influence of lute writing appears suddenly in the *Firste Pavian,* to remain part of Byrd's idiom and to lend grace to all keyboard writing. Experiments of many kinds lead to a true virtuosic style, to be further developed musically and technically by John Bull, Orlando Gibbons, Giles Farnaby and Thomas Tomkins.

The Nevill manuscript is an important document, a landmark in the history of keyboard music. For the student readying himself for Bach and the eighteenth century, there is no comparable preparation. For the teacher given to starting with Bach and Scarlatti, it is a revelation, for they are the culmination. Here is the source.

1968 BLANCHE WINOGRON

[9] Since 1926 a quantity of materials earlier than, contemporary with and immediately subsequent to *My Ladye Nevells Booke* has been discovered, and some published:

45 Pieces for Keyboard Instruments . . . , ed. Stephen D. Tuttle, Paris, [*c.* 1939].

Will Forster's Virginal Book, ed. Edmund H. Fellowes, London, 1950.

The Mulliner Book (*Musica Britannica,* Vol. I), ed. Denis Stevens, London, 1951.

The Dublin Virginal Manuscript, ed. John Ward, Wellesley, 1954.

The Keyboard Music of Thomas Tomkins (*Musica Britannica,* Vol. 5), ed. Stephen D. Tuttle, London, 1955.

Clement Matchett's Virginal Book, ed. Thurston Dart, London, 1957.

The Kinloch Manuscript (*Musica Britannica,* Vol. 15), ed. Kenneth Elliott, London, 1957.

The Keyboard Music of John Bull (*Musica Britannica,* Vol. 14 and 19), edd. John Steele and Francis Cameron, and Thurston Dart, London, 1960 and 1963.

The Keyboard Music of Orlando Gibbons (*Musica Britannica,* Vol. 20), ed. Gerald Hendrie, London, 1962.

Priscilla Bunbury's Virginal Book, ed. John L. Boston, London, 1962.

Elizabeth Rogers Virginal Book, selection ed. Frank Dawes, Mainz, n.d.

Lady Jean Campbell's Virginal Manuscript.

There are also several relevant manuscripts in the Paris Bibliothèque Nationale, the Vienna Nationalbibliothek, etc.

ACKNOWLEDGMENTS

I HAVE first of all to acknowledge with grateful thanks the generosity of Lord Henry Nevill, to whom I am indebted for permission to transcribe, edit, and publish *My Ladye Nevells Booke*, and for the many courtesies and kindnesses extended to me while working on the manuscript at Eridge Castle. To Sir Richard Terry, well known as one of the fathers of the Tudor Music revival, to whose long years at Westminster Cathedral Tudor music owes its living appeal, I owe a debt that I can never repay, for the inspiration and limitless kindness that I have always received from him, and for the help that he lavishes upon interested students. In the preparation of this edition for publication I should have been at a loss without his advice. My thanks are due to Professor Granville Bantock for his initial help and suggestions; and to Miss Margaret H. Glyn, whose deep knowledge of virginal music makes her advice particularly valuable, for her interest in this edition and for the loan of her photographs of the Drexel MS. in the New York Public Library. Acknowledgments are due to the Bibliothécaire of the Conservatoire de Musique in Paris for permission to consult manuscripts and to edit and publish in this edition two short extracts; and to the Dean of Christ Church, Oxford, for permission to refer to manuscripts in the Library there.

Reference to Mr. Gerald Cooper's valuable thematic card-index enabled me to locate a string version of one of the pieces in *My Ladye Nevells Booke*. I am much indebted to Mr. A. I. Ellis for help in reading proofs, and to my other friends at the British Museum, who have furthered my research work there in many ways.

HILDA ANDREWS

London, June 1926

PREFACE

OUR national habit of self-depreciation has never been more curiously exhibited than in our treatment of early British composers.

The Elizabethan madrigal, after a short vogue of thirty years, entered on three centuries of eclipse. The greatest church music of the Tudor period disappeared altogether. That we ever had early instrumental music which was neither empirical nor of mere academic interest, is only now beginning to be realized. In this connexion we so complacently accepted the superficial dicta of historians (that no English keyboard music of artistic value existed before Purcell), that the publication of *The Fitzwilliam Virginal Book* in 1899 (which came as a great surprise to students) may be regarded as an historic event. In the same category we must place Miss Andrews' transcription of *My Ladye Nevells Booke*.

In the history of other nations the gradual rise and development of music—from comparative crudity to ultimate perfection—can be readily traced. But in Tudor England, the sudden efflorescence of full-blown art forms is a phenomenon that lacks a parallel, unless it be the troubadour music of Provence.

The supremacy of William Byrd in vocal composition is now receiving belated recognition. Miss Andrews' work is therefore welcome as furnishing evidence (hitherto confined to a few students) that this supremacy held good in instrumental music as well. It also brings into stronger relief the fact (already noted by Charles van den Borren and Margaret Glyn) that the source of modern keyboard technique is to be found in English virginal music—that so far from being followers of other nations, we were really pioneers.

To her task Miss Andrews brings not only ripe scholarship and critical insight, but a lively artistic sympathy without which the highest academic credentials prove barren. It is with confidence that we look to such editors for still further evidence that in Byrd and his contemporaries we have music that is alive and not dead. It is in labours of love like the present that we may hope for the speedy restoration of our national musical heritage, and the recapture of its very distinctive æsthetic appeal.

R. R. TERRY

Original binding of My Ladye Nevells Booke (*reduced*)

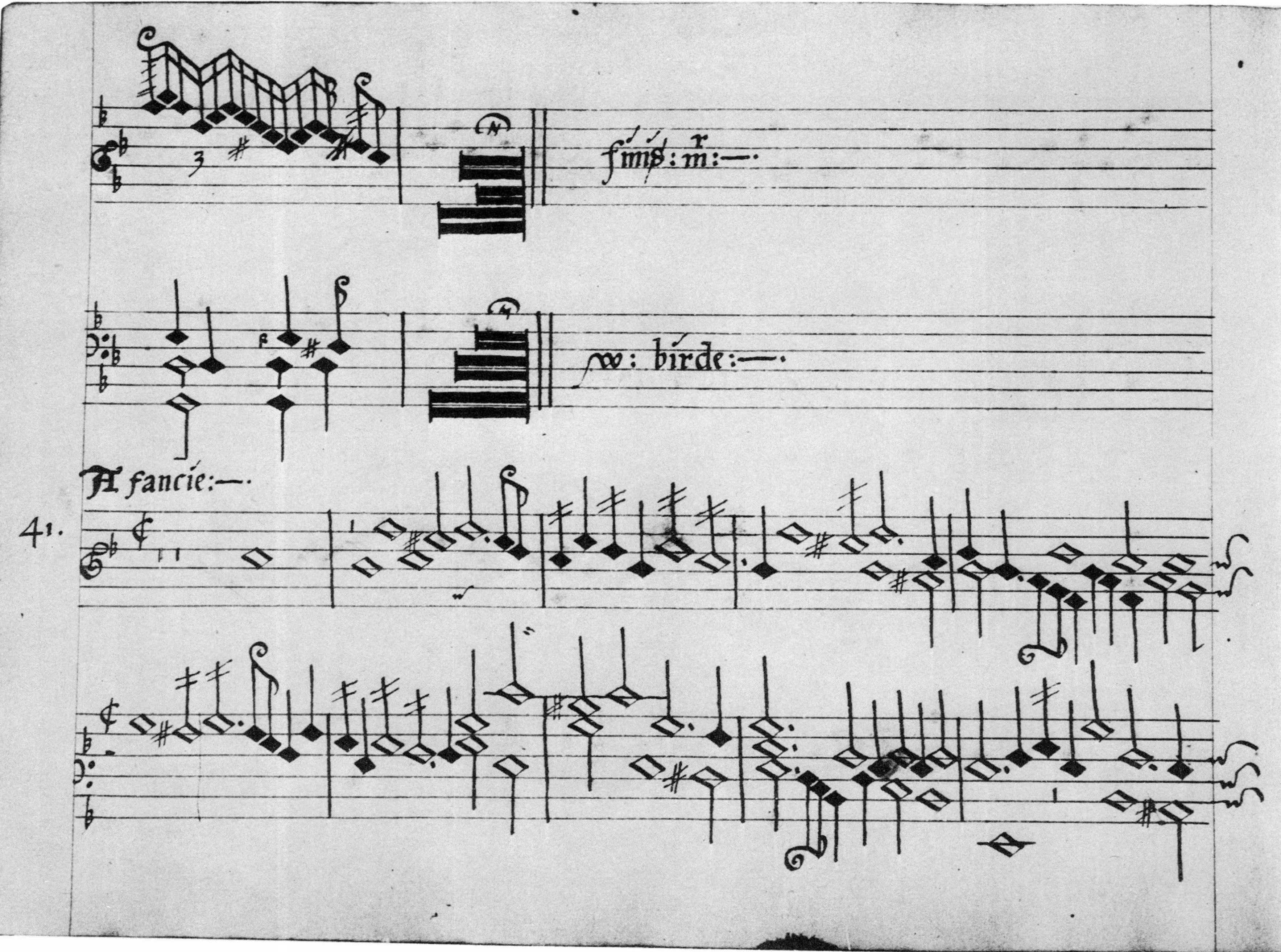

Facsimile page from My Ladye Nevells Booke

56.

Facsimile page from My Ladye Nevells Booke

will yow walke the woodes soe wylde:—

.109.

Facsimile page from My Ladye Nevells Booke

CONTENTS

MUSIC

CONTENTS—*continued*

MY LADYE NEVELLS BOOKE 1591

HISTORICAL NOTE

AFTER three centuries of neglect the secular instrumental art of William Byrd is coming into its own. Recent editions of string pieces by him reveal a vein of surprising individuality in a direction long unrecognized. Until quite lately his far more important music for the virginal has received that due meed of grudging attention usually accorded to work whose true quality lies below the surface and is little understood. Even among students of the Tudor period, intimately versed in Byrd's vocal music, ecclesiastical and secular, his keyboard work has rarely had adequate recognition on æsthetic grounds. Yet there survives in MS. a mass of his keyboard compositions, half of them already edited; MS. texts of his virginal lessons are both more numerous and more accurate than of any other of the great virginalists, so that fragmentary evidence cannot be offered as an excuse. Such popular neglect may be partly explained in the circumstance that existing sources[1] of information in modern notation, though extensive and valuable, provide an unwieldy collection of Byrd's work, lacking cohesion, and by no means wholly representative of his many-sided genius—a disproportionate collection in which his best work happens to fall largely into one style, including an unfair proportion of lessons that are as artistically uninspired and dull as they are historically interesting. In such work the pioneer dominates the artist. It is consequently not altogether surprising that misapprehensions should have arisen, and values been assigned to him, not false, but half-true. It is too often the lot of the pioneer in any branch of art that posterity is inclined to remember him for his position in the history of art rather than for his intrinsic gifts to it. The significance of manner overwhelms the wider significance of matter. Students of Byrd's virginal music have been obsessed with the importance of his technical achievement in the development of keyboard style, in the creation of keyboard music as a form as

[1] The chief source is the *Fitzwilliam Virginal Book*, edited by Fuller-Maitland and Squire, in which there are seventy-two pieces by Byrd. For a complete list of other sources, *vide infra*, p. xxxvii.

cultured as the madrigal and motett, to the extent of letting the inherent musical beauty of his work in that same novel style slide into comparative insignificance. Certainly, it is hardly possible to overestimate the importance of his work from this aspect; nevertheless it is one that will always make a stronger appeal to the scholar and antiquary than to the average listener, to whom it is naturally a matter of little account, and to whom the purely æsthetic aspect is all-important.

The sheer dynamic impetus of Byrd's musical genius forced him right outside the rhythmic and tonal limitations that were rapidly becoming a constraining influence upon the art. In purely polyphonic vocal music he conforms to the existing vocal style, working within the confines of a musical scheme inherited from his predecessors and in slow process of evolution. In the self-imposed task of creating a technique of composition for the virginal he breaks abruptly away into a freer idiom. There is between the embryonic art of Hugh Aston [1] and the polished vigour of Byrd a wider gulf, technically and in every other way, than between Byrd and Bach, though the earlier virginalist only preceded Byrd by fifty years. Analysing Byrd's methods, one finds that the new technique is dependent upon the advent into written music of regular rhythm. How, it will later be shown; for the moment, the essential point to be made clear is that Byrd's work for the virginal is approximately based on two fundamentally opposed factors, the old tradition of polyphony—out of which developed the free fantasia, the strict Continental *ricercare*, and ultimately the fugue—and the innovation of regular accent, involved by the exigencies of court-dance and folk-song. The latter element predominates in his best-known work, in pieces like 'The Carmans Whistle' and 'Sellingers Round.' But it is too little realized that his most intrinsically beautiful work was produced when the robust vigour of accented rhythm was present as an influence allied to and revitalizing the old serious sweetness of the contrapuntal style. It is here that the artist dominates the pioneer, and little is generally known of his work in this vein except the 'Pavan and Galliard—the Earle of Salisbury' from *Parthenia*.[2] Yet this is no isolated example. The presence of a genuine anthology of Byrd's virginal music, which we are fortunate enough to possess in *My Ladye Nevells Booke*, should make it possible to correct a rather one-sided impression and to construct from it a true

[1] *Circa* 1510.

[2] *Parthenia*, the first printed music for the virginal, 1611.

estimate of his work from every standpoint, seeing that *My Ladye Nevells Booke* preserves an even balance between the various phases of his style. The superficial charm of Byrd's virginal music lies in a delicacy of detail and nuance, unemotional and placid, but an intimate study of his best work reveals the depths of its grave and enduring beauty, and the splendid vitality of his inventive faculty, never surpassed and rarely equalled by any of his contemporaries.

This manuscript, *My Ladye Nevells Booke*, is still preserved at Eridge Castle in Sussex, the seat of the Marquess of Abergavenny, to whose ancestor, the little-known but musicianly Lady Nevell whose name it bears, it was given in 1591.[1] Written in the script of John Baldwin, the famous scribe of Windsor, it is generally acknowledged to be one of the finest Tudor MSS. extant. Circumstances have protected it from the careless hands of casual inquirers, and even during the hundred odd years when it lapsed from its proper owners, it has never been easily accessible, a treasure only to be handled by a privileged few, essentially a masterpiece of craftsmanship, with its old beauty still unspoilt, its clear script still bright. As a 'named variety' it is unique among virginal MSS. There must have been many similar collections long since lost, bearing famous names, like *The Earl of Leicester's Book*, mentioned by Rimbault in his 1847 edition of *Parthenia*, but of all these there is no trace. *My Ladye Nevells Booke* alone survives to mark the custom of compiling collections of virginal lessons for distinguished patrons, a custom as universal in the sixteenth century as the acquisition by cultured people of a 'consort of viols'.

Briefly described, the Nevell MS. is a heavy oblong folio volume, and although the original binding has since been discreetly repaired, it retains exactly its original appearance (*vide* photographs of binding and script), the old binding and backing having been ingeniously and carefully replaced on the top of the new. The back and front covers are identical, of brown morocco elaborately tooled with gold and enriched with colour, red and green. The lining of faded blue watered silk is of more recent date. On the title-page is the coat-of-arms of the Nevill family, illuminated, with the monogram H. N. in the lower left-hand corner. This, again, does not date back as far as 1591. There are 192 folios of script, four six-lined staves

[1] That it was a gift is a conjecture, certainly, but a safe one. Lady Nevell must have been closely associated with Byrd and, whether as pupil or patron, it was undoubtedly written for her.

to a page, the notes large and diamond-shaped, and at the end an accurate table of contents, 'the table for this booke', with the following colophon appended—'finished & ended the leventh of September in the yeare of our Lord God 1591 & in the 33 yeare of the raigne of our sofferaine ladie Elizabeth by the grace of God queene of Englande etc, by me Jo. Baldwine of Windsore. Laus deo.'

The history of the book is curious and involved. Pasted on the flyleaf is a MS. note in a seventeenth-century hand, evidently that of a later member of the family, tracing the history of the MS. from its original owner in 1591 through its wandering course till 1668.

> 'This Book was presented to Queene Elizabeth by my Lord Edward Abergevenny called the Deafe, the queene ordered one S^r^. or M^r^. North one of her servants to keepe it, who left it to his son who gave it Mr. Haughton Attorny of Cliffords Inn & he last somer 1668 gave it to me; this mr. North as I remember Mr. haughton saide, was uncle to the last L^d^. North.
>
> H. Bergevenny'

From 1668 until the end of the eighteenth century it was apparently preserved among the treasures of the Nevill family without a break. The next definite record of it occurs in the catalogue of Dr. Burney's library, sold after his death in 1814. The reference is unmistakable, but how it came to be in his possession is not stated and the problem is still unsolved. It may have been lent and subsequently given to him as a very famous musician and antiquary. In his *History of Music* (1776–89), he several times refers to the MS., but is curiously uncommunicative on the point of ownership, though details are minute enough to lead one to suspect that at the time of writing it was, temporarily at least, in his possession. At the sale of his books on August 11, 1814, it was Lot 561, and was acquired by Thomas Jones, of Nottingham Place, a discerning and enthusiastic collector, for £11 0s. 6d. When Jones's library was sold twelve years later on February 15th, 1826, the MS. was Lot 342, and was bought by Robert Triphook, a bibliophile and bookseller of St. James's Street. By him it was sold back to Lord Abergavenny; the exact date cannot be traced, as when Triphook gave up his business in 1833 *My Ladye Nevells Booke* was not in the sale catalogue and must have been sold by private treaty some time before. Triphook seems to have been a curiously interesting old man and, had he left any account of the book, might conceivably have thrown light on the subject of its acquisition by Dr. Burney, now the only missing link in its history.

Exhaustive research for chance reference to the MS. in eighteenth- and nineteenth-century periodicals has cleared up certain doubtful points, but yields no further clue. Since it was acquired from Triphook the book has remained in the Nevill family.

The historical record would be incomplete without some explanation of the widespread confusion that existed in the middle of the nineteenth century between *My Ladye Nevells Booke* and another MS., then generally supposed to be the original. This MS., now in the British Museum,[1] possibly contemporary, or more probably of a little later date, is labelled on what is now the title-page, 'Extracts from Virginal Book, Lady Nevil's: Tallis. Byrd. Bull. etc.' It also was once the property of Thomas Jones and was sold at the sale of his library, passing afterwards into the hands of Dr. E. F. Rimbault. There is no reason to doubt its containing *bona fide* copies from the Nevell MS., since it includes thirteen pieces from it, written in an unskilled script and with many copyist's 'improvements'; there are also pieces by other composers than Byrd. This preliminary explanation will perhaps make the position clearer. The following correspondence must now be quoted from some early numbers of *Notes and Queries*, between Dr. E. F. Rimbault, Mr. William Chappell, the musical antiquary, and an enigmatic L. B. L.

Notes and Queries, Vol. VII, Jan. 15, 1853. *Lady Nevill's Music Book.*

The following contents of the *Lady Nevill's Music Book*[2] (1591) may be interesting to many of your readers:—[follows the table of contents at the end of Nevell MS.]. The songs have no words to them. Most of the airs are signed 'Mr. William Byrde.' A modern MS. note[3] in the book states that the book is 'Lady Nevill's Music Book' and that she seems 'to have been the scholar of Birde, who professedly composed several of these pieces for her ladyship's use,' and that 'Jo. Baldwin was a singing man of Windsor'.

The music is written on four-stave paper of six lines, in large bold characters, with great neatness. The notes are lozenge-shaped. Can any

[1] B.M. Additional MS. 30485.

[2] By the description this is obviously the original *My Ladye Nevells Booke.*

[3] This note has evidently been lost, as there is now no trace of it. It was probably Burney's.

of your correspondents furnish rules for transposing these six-line staves into the five-line staves of modern notations? L. B. L.

Feb. 19, 1853.
Lady Nevill's Music-book.
[Instructions for transposition of six-line staves, etc.]

I should feel greatly obliged to your correspondent L. B. L. for a sight of this Virginal Book as it appears to be an exact transcript of the one in Dr. Rimbault's possession. Wm. Chappell, 201 Regent Street.

Feb. 26, 1853.
Lady Nevill's Music Bk.

The index to *Lady Nevill's Music Book* printed by your correspondent L. B. L. was made known to the public in 1789 in the third volume of Dr. Burney's *History of Music*. The MS. in question was the property of Dr. Burney, at whose sale in 1814 it was purchased for £10 10s. by Mr. Thomas Jones, of Nottingham Place. At the sale of the latter about ten years later, it was bought by Triphook the bookseller and by him sold to Lord Abergavenny. I remember seeing the book when in Triphook's possession, since which time I had lost sight of it until the notice by L. B. L. in your pages. Mr. Thomas Jones was a well-known musical antiquarian, and possessed many rare treasures in this department. One of the most important was the *original* MS. of *Lady Nevill's Music Book*, in the handwriting of William Byrd the composer. This valuable relic is now in my library. John Baldwine, the person who made the splendid copy for the use of Lady Nevill, was a singular character. I have some materials for his biography which may one day see light. He was a poet in his own time and wrote a metrical account of famous musicians. . . . Edward F. Rimbault.

The Byrd autograph is patently a wild flight of imagination. If Rimbault's statements were accurate it would imply the existence of *three* MSS. called *Lady Nevill's Book,* of which the 'original Byrd autograph', of vital interest, was regarded by Rimbault as of so little importance that it was disposed of during his lifetime and lost to sight; there is no mention of such a book in the catalogue of his library, which includes only the inferior MS. *Extracts from Lady Nevil's Book.* This public correspondence must have elicited the truth of the matter: Chappell himself was no meticulously accurate scholar, but in him at least there was no guile, and on examination he must have seen at once that the 'interesting relic' was no original Byrd autograph. At all events one hears no more of it. Only six years later, in his 1859 edition of *Popular Music of the Olden Time*, Chappell acknowledges the loan of *My Lady Nevells Booke* from Lord Abergavenny, mentioning no other, though Rimbault's own copious notes on folk-tunes and his entire library were at his disposal for reference, and must have included the Byrd autograph Nevell MS., an important source, had it existed.

In a publication[1] of the next year Rimbault claims the ownership of *Lady Nevill's Book*, and at the same time affords undeniable proof that the MS. in question was not the original, but the book of Extracts. Other evidence of the same type leads to the inevitable conclusion that it is wisest to dispense with his opinions altogether, since it is impossible to reconcile them with conflicting facts of unassailable authenticity. The unfortunate result of such confusion was that some of the earlier dictionaries, Fétis, and even Riemann, described the inferior MS. for the original, evidently basing their information on Rimbault's description and knowing nothing of the original *My Ladye Nevells Booke*, long hidden in an obscurity from which it is only now emerging.

John Baldwin, scribe, musician and scholar, dismissed briefly in nearly all the earlier records as 'a singing man of Windsor' or 'gentleman of the Chapel Royal', must have been a distinguished though unobtrusive personality, overshadowed by his more brilliant contemporaries and of comparative insignificance in the musical world of his day. The Cheque Book of the Chapel Royal is the only source of information about his career, giving the date of his appointment there and of his death in 1615.

> 3 Feby. 1593-4. that John Bauldwyne of the college of wynsor should be placed next in ordynarye in Her Majesties Chapple, the former promyses made to any other notwithstandinge . . .
>
> Leonard Davies.
>
> 23 March 1594.
>
> The Rt. Hon. the Lord Chamberlaine gave me order to sware John Bauldwin (named before in this page) gentleman in ordinary (without pay) in her Majesties Chappell, and until a tenor's place be voyde, & then

[1] *A History of the Pianoforte*, by E. F. Rimbault, 1860.

he to have & be sworne with wages for the firste & nexte tenor that shalbe admitted & placed in her Highness chappell, noe man whatsoever to prevent him . . .

Leonard Davies
Sub dean.

1598 Robert Tallentire died the 15th of August & John Baldwin sworne in his place the 25th of the same from Winsor.

1615 John Baldwin died the 28th of August and Martin Otto was sworne in his place.

Baldwin's fine script has come down to us first of all in *My Ladye Nevells Booke*, 'finished and ended' in 1591, when he was still a lay-clerk of St. George's Chapel, Windsor, in the famous collection of motetts and instrumental pieces in the Royal Library[1], not finished till more than ten years later, in an incomplete set of part-books[2] of which the tenor book is lacking, in the Library at Christ Church, Oxford, and in one of a set of part-books at the Music School, Oxford.[3]

In the motett collection in the Royal Library there are seventeen of Baldwin's own compositions, largely instrumental pieces of the fantasia type, including a three-part setting of the popular 'Browning' tune—'the leaves bee greene'. These are of a quality to place him at once in a totally different class from the ordinary slipshod scribe of the time. At the end of the same MS. is appended a rambling account by Baldwin of the English and Continental masters of music, written in quaint couplets.[4] Hawkins, in

[1] On permanent loan to the British Museum.

[2] Ch.Ch. MSS. 979-83

[3] Bodleian Library, Forrest-Heather Collection, Mus. Sch. MSS. e. 376-381.

[4] 'Reede here, behold and see all that musicions bee;
What is inclosde herein, declare I will begine.
A storehousse of treasure this booke may be saiede
Of songes most excelente and the beste that is made,
Collected and chosen out of the best autours
Both strainger and English borne, which bee the best makers
And skilfulst in musicke, the scyence to sett forthe
As herein you shall finde if you will speake the truthe.
There is here no badd songe, but the best cann be hadd,
The chiefest from all men; yea there is not one badd,
And such sweet musicke as dothe much delite yeilde
Both unto men at home and birds abroade in fielde.

his *History of Music,* calls the verse homely, as he might well do, but finds it interesting as a contemporary opinion of the great Tudor contrapuntalists. Baldwin, though no poet, was a discriminating critic, evidently well versed in the music of his day, both at home and abroad. He must have been intimately associated with Byrd, for whom he had a boundless admiration, as these same verses show, and in *My Ladye Nevells Booke* he names him 'homo memorabilis'. The Christ Church part-books contain motetts and string pieces, and were probably his own property, bearing the initials 'I. B.' on the cover. There are four of his own compositions, instrumental pieces, in the collection, all incomplete owing to the missing tenor book.

The Forrest-Heather Collection at the Music School provides only thirteen folios in his inimitable script, signed with the inevitable 'Jo. Baldwine, laus deo'. He held no unworthy position in that erudite age of English music; but beyond this fact history is barren of any record. Rimbault claimed to have material for his biography, and it would be interesting to know if he had access to any more productive sources of information, but in any case they are now lost beyond recall. The elusive personality of the 'singing man of Windsor' has faded into an insubstantial creature of the imagination.

Turning to the substance of *My Ladye Nevells Booke*, a close examination proves it to be a unique document, and Baldwin's part in it of considerable significance. It contains in the forty-two pieces a representative collection of Byrd's keyboard work, enough for us to form an adequate estimate of his style independent of any further evidence. Among existing MSS. it is

The autours for to name I maye not here forgett,
But will them now downe put and all in order sett.
I will begine with White, Shepper, Tye and Tallis,
Parsons, Gyles, Mundie th'oulde one of the queenes pallis,
Mundie yonge, th'oulde mans sonne and like wyse others moe;
There names would be to longe, therefore I let them goe;
Yet must I speake of moe even of straingers also;
And firste I must bringe in Alfonso Ferabosco,
A strainger borne he was ain Italie as I here;
Italians saie of him in skill he had no peere.
Luca Merensio with others manie moe,
As Philipp Demonte the Emperours man also;
And Orlando by name and eeke Crequillion,
Cipriano Rore: and also Andreon.
All famous in there arte, there is of that no doute:
There workes no lesse declare in everie place aboute,

an isolated instance of a virginal book of a composer's selected lessons written in a uniformly careful hand. Moreover, everything points to the fact that Baldwin was copying from Byrd's own MS., and the resulting text is consequently as far removed as it could well be from the average MS. of the period, packed with the accumulated mistakes and 'improvements' of one inept scribe after another. An authority on Tudor and later virginal music ascribes[1] the importance of the Nevell MS. as a text to the probability that it was corrected by Byrd himself, and certainly the various minor additions and trivial corrections that appear in the text from time to time in a strange script seem to indicate the composer's hand. Beyond doubt this script is not Baldwin's, and it seems reasonable to suppose it to have been Byrd's, though it might conceivably have been a later writer's work. But substantially the responsibility for the accuracy of the text lies with Baldwin, and I prefer to emphasize this and to suggest that his scholarship alone was enough to ensure the entire reliability of the copy. The existence of so authoritative a text is of signal importance in the consideration of variant readings in other MSS., and particularly in dealing with the vexed question of *musica ficta*. The Nevell MS. reading can in all cases be assumed to be the original one. It is also considerably the earliest text of Byrd's keyboard music and, indeed, of any virginal music of the great school, the next important one being twenty years later. Even *The*

Yet let not straingers bragg, nor they these soe commende,
For they may now geve place and sett themselves behynde,
An Englishman, by name, William Birde for his skill.
Which I should heve sett first, for soe it was my will,
Whose greater skill and knowledge dothe excelle all at this tyme
And far to strange countries abroade his skill dothe shyne;
Famous men be abroad, and skilful in the arte
I do confesse the fame and not from it starte;
But in Ewroppe is none like to our Englishe man,
Which dothe so farre exceede, as trulie I it scan
As ye cannot finde out his equale in all thinges
Throwghe out the worlde so wide, and so his fame now ringes.
With fingers and with penne he hathe not now his peere;
For in this worlde so wide is none can him come neere,
The rarest man he is in musicks worthy arte
That now on earthe doth liue: I speake it from my harte
Or heere to fore hath been or after him shall come
None suche I feare shall rise that may be calde his sonne.

[1] Miss M. H. Glyn, in *Elizabethan Virginal Music and Composers* (William Reeves).

Fitzwilliam Book, the most valuable because the most extensive source of virginal music, is copied from MSS. of widely varying dates, and contains many mutilated versions, occupying as an accurate text a very secondary position to *My Ladye Nevells Booke.*

The cultivated technique of virginal music that came suddenly into being at the end of the sixteenth century owed so little to tradition and so much to its founder, William Byrd, that it was virtually a new creation. The earlier virginal compositions were of a crude and undeveloped character, of little intrinsic value, with barely a promise of the achievement to come. Hugh Aston, whose name is found in *My Ladye Nevells Booke* in the piece called 'Hugh Ashtons Grownde', was Byrd's earliest predecessor, and flourished fifty years before. Unfortunately, there is little record of his or of contemporary work for the virginal—only enough to show that sporadic attempts were being made to develop keyboard music on definite lines, though it was then of the most primitive type. The only surviving piece for the virginal by Aston is a 'hornepype' in a British Museum MS.,[1] which contains other contemporary keyboard pieces of great historical interest, among them an anonymous composer's 'My Ladye Careys Dompe', which also may be cited as an example of this primitive work. Aston's 'hornepype' is a crude piece, built up on the simplest possible harmonic basis, of vigour, immense length and little else. 'My Ladye Careys Dompe' is an effort at variation-form, but of so rudimentary a type that it does no more than foreshadow the advanced instrumental writing of the great school of

O famous man! of skill and judgemente great profounde
Lett heaven and earth ringe out they worthye praise to sounde;
Ney lett they skill itselfe they worthie fame recorde
To all posteritie they due desert afforde;
And lett them all which heere of thy greate skill then saie
Fare well, fare well thou prince of musicke now and aye;
Fare well I say fare well, fare well and here end
Fare well melodious Birde, fare well sweet musickes frende
All these thinges do I speake not for rewarde or bribe;
Nor yet to flatter him or sett him upp in pride
Nor for affection or ought might move there towe
But euen the truth reporte and that make known to yowe
Lo! heere I end farewell committing all to God . . .
Who kepe us in his grace and shilde us from his rodd.'

Finis Jo. Baldwine.

[1] Royal Appendix 58.

virginalists. Yet one finds in both pieces traces of later technique in figuration like spread chords—which, of course, abound in the later work—rapid scale passages and little rhythmic figures repeated sequentially, all distinctly virginalistic in style.

Other pieces in this MS. furnish no further evidence of the technique of this early work. But it must be recognized that Hugh Aston and his contemporaries were groping their way to an independent technique of composition for the virginal quite distinct from the contrapuntal work for voices or the organ. These English pieces are, moreover, the earliest known virginal compositions in existence, and though one finds them intrinsically tedious and uninteresting, historically they mark an epoch.

After Hugh Aston, there is only the record of the famous *Mulliner Book*[1] to bridge the half-century till *My Ladye Nevells Booke* was written. The *Mulliner Book* consists of pieces by the mid-sixteenth-century organist-composers, Redford, Blitheman, and their contemporaries, most of them apparently for the organ and written in the contrapuntal style with little rhythmic interest, many adapted from vocal pieces, or fantasias upon plainsong. These organ compositions afford no evidence of any actual advance of rhythmic technique for the virginal, only of the polyphonic organ style. In two or three instances of plainsong variations by Redford and Blitheman one finds a vaguely rhythmic character and some florid virginalistic ornament in the form of scale passages, but no further development beyond that shown in Aston's 'hornepype'. Tallis's 'Felix Namque' (1564), in the *Fitzwilliam Book*,[2] exemplifies this simple fantasia type in a rather more developed stage. The only piece in the Mulliner MS. that does more than hint at the future growth of an independent secular style is a little neglected 'pavyon' by Newman, written, though very simply, in a definite dance-form.

Between Aston and Byrd, therefore, there is practically no link. After Byrd, the other great virginalists, Gibbons, Bull, and Farnaby, his younger contemporaries, added nothing to the style he had initiated beyond a further elaboration of superficial ornament, a convention which was later to become a veneer to hide a certain decadence of inspiration. Sprung full-grown from Byrd's infinite musical resource, the new music, both the system on which it was based and the style in which it materialized, was of a type

[1] The *Mulliner Book*, British Museum Additional MS. 30513.
[2] *Fitzwilliam Book*, modern edition, Vol. II, p. 1.

hitherto unimagined, evolved from a medley of conflicting influences unconsciously gathered together and moulded into a coherent form by the sure instinct of genius. The free style now initiated by Byrd imposed upon the old flexible horizontal polyphony—the natural basis of all Tudor music for voices, viols, and organ—two closely related elements new to 'pricked' music, of a purely secular origin, quite foreign to the prevailing classical standards. The two points are mutually dependent, the second subordinated to and arising from the first, the new sense of regularly accented rhythm involving inevitably a vertical conception of harmony, or, rather, a conception of harmony as a function of music distinct from melody, and not, as it had hitherto been conceived, incidental to melody. The all-pervasive influence of folk-song and the elevation of the dance into an art form, introduced now into written music for the first time as a rhythmic foundation and an integral part of it, brought regular accent; the growing harmonic sense found its precedent in the tendencies of the lutenist school, already progressing on empirical lines towards defined harmony, which the very nature of the lute made the only possible direction for development. The large part played by the lutenist school at this point in shaping the course of musical technique is of infinite importance. The perfectly balanced counterpoint of polyphony gave place to accompanied monody, and the purely empirical methods of the lute-players, half-a-century ahead of their time, were the controlling influence upon the secular art.

The radical advance effected in virginal music by the fusion of the old style with the new can be observed at its highest point in the many examples of court-dance and variation-form, brought at the outset by Byrd to a pitch of excellence that was never surpassed, the latter in its many aspects perhaps the most significant of the virginalistic forms that then attained instant popularity.

Bearing in mind, therefore, that in virginal music generally and in Byrd's particularly there are at work two main forces, the tradition of vocal polyphony and the revolutionary factor of accented rhythm, new to written music, the various forms are easily analysable, influenced in varying degrees by one or other of these basic principles.

The fantasia as a form approximates to the contrapuntal style, the forerunner of the later pianoforte fugues. The form varies: there are many that develop after a purely *fugato* opening section into countless 'divisions'[1]

[1] Florid decorations of melody.

and episodes of a distinctly virginalistic type showing the superficial growth of florid ornament for brilliant effects of execution; others, plain-song fantasias and keyboard *In Nomines,*[1] are entirely contrapuntal, adapted in short score from viol pieces and often uninteresting, not far enough removed from the purely vocal style to have acquired individuality. On the other hand, in the court-dance forms—the origin of the suite—the rhythmic element predominates. Byrd's famous contemporary, Thomas Morley, gives in his *Plaine and Easie Introduction to Practicall Music*[2] a detailed description of these instrumental forms, so precise that further comment is unnecessary.

'The most principall and chiefest kind of music which is made without a dittie is the fantasie, that is when a musician taketh a point at his pleasure and wresteth it and turneth it as he list, making either much or little of it according as shal seem best in his own conceit. In this may more art be shown than in any other music, because the composer is tied to nothing but that he may add diminish and alter at his pleasure . . . The next in gravitie and goodness unto this is called a pavan a kind of staid music ordained for grave dauncing, and most commonly made of three straines, whereof everie strain is plaid or sung twice: a straine they make to contain 8, 12, or 16 semibriefs as they list, yet fewer than eight I have not seene in any pavan. In this you may not so much insist in following the point as in a fantasia: but it shd be enough to touch it once and so away to some close. Also in this you must cast your musicke by foure: so that if you keepe that rule it is no matter how manie foures you put into your straine: for it wil fall out wel enough in the end: the art of dancing being come to that perfection that everie reasonable dancer will make measure of no measure, so that it is no great matter of what number you make your straine. After every pavan we usually set a galliard (that is a kind of musick made out of the other) causing it to go by a measure, which the learned call trochaicam rationem, consisting of a long and short stroke successively: for as the foot trochaeus consisting of one syllable of two times, and another of one time, so is the first of these two strokes double to the latter, the first being in the time of a semibriefe and the latter of a minime. This is a lighter and more stirring kind of dancing than the pavan consisting of the same number of straines: and look how

[1] Fantasias upon the plainsong 'Gloria Tibi Trinitas.'
[2] Published in 1597.

many foures of semibriefes you put in the straine of your pavan, so many times sixe minims must you put in the straine of your galliard . . .

'The Alman is a more heavie daunce than this, so that no extraordinary motions are used in dauncing of it. It is made of strains sometimes two, sometimes three, and everie strain is made by four: but you must mark that the four of the pavan measure is in dupla proportion to the four of the alman measure; so that as the usual pavan containeth in a strain the time of sixteen semibriefes so the usual alman containeth the time of eight and most commonly in short notes . . .

'There also be many other kinds of dances (as hornepypes, Jygges and infinite more) which I cannot nominate unto you: but knowing these, the rest cannot but be understood, as being one with some of these which I have already told you.'

The variation-form explains itself, and includes variations, sometimes rhythmic and harmonic, sometimes contrapuntal, on folk-song and dance tunes, grounds, and the six notes, *ut, re, mi, fa, sol, la,* of the hexachord, though the last is nearer in effect to the plainsong fantasia, a form very much used for strings and the earlier organ and virginal music. Folk-tune variations and grounds followed very much the same lines, the tune being many times varied, simple at first and growing in complexity and brilliance towards the end. The ground of Elizabethan music is not always the strict ground-bass of modern use: it implies merely a short theme subject to variation and may appear in any part. A feature of the contrapuntal variation-form is the 'tripla' counterpoint that inevitably appears in the course of a piece as the musical web grows more complex, sometimes involving intricate cross rhythms with the theme. Such tripla variations often take the form of fragments of folk-tune, and even where the melodies cannot actually be traced, the folk-song idiom is apparent. Byrd frequently uses this form of ornamental development in the fantasia, taking a short tripla theme and working it out as a contrapuntal figure in free fugue. His use of it in hexachord variations can be seen in the 'ut, re, mi, fa, sol, la,' in *My Ladye Nevells Booke.* A far more interesting example is afforded by another hexachord piece, a later work of Byrd's, in a MS. in the Library at the Paris Conservatoire[1] de Musique. Here there are five variations on the hexachord, the last three of which consist of an ingenious treatment of the folk-tunes, 'The Woodes soe Wylde' and 'The Shaking of the Sheets'; both

[1] Paris Conservatoire MS. 18547, the autograph of Thomas Tomkins.

melodies are used complete, and interwoven with every contrapuntal device, elaborately extended and developed. The piece is technically superior to the comparatively simple hexachord variations in *My Ladye Nevells Booke,* and is an illuminating instance of Byrd's use of folk-song. It is interesting, too, to note that his treatment of 'The Woodes soe Wylde' tune in the hexachord piece is purely contrapuntal, and his variations on it in *My Ladye Nevells Booke* purely rhythmic. But whether used as a rhythmic basis for variation or as contrapuntal embroidery of other thematic material, folk-song is demonstrably an influence everywhere at work in the formation of virginalistic technique.

The diatonic system on which this virginal music was based may be said to bridge the gulf between modality and modern tonality. English folk-tunes lie in the Ionian, Dorian, Aeolian, and Mixolydian modes, the majority being cast in the Ionian mode, which exactly approximates with its natural sharpened seventh to our modern major scale. The chromatic alteration of the seventh in the Mixolydian mode makes it identical with the Ionian in order of intervals. The widespread popularity in secular music of tunes in this natural major mode—the *modus lascivus,* not encouraged in music for the Church—showed itself in the trend of fashion, in lute music especially, toward the use of the sharpened seventh in all modes, and consequently in the direction of a more or less uniform scale, and towards the narrowing down[1] of the elaborate modal system, with its equally elaborate system of *musica ficta*, to the two modes of modern use. The Dorian and Aeolian modes, for example, need only the sharpened seventh to bring them closely into line with our minor mode. With this tendency towards the universal use of the sharpened seventh, the uncertainty of the tonic in modal music gradually gave place to the definite sense of leading note and tonic, and ultimately to tonality as we know it. But in this transitional, wholly experimental, period there was no divorce between the major and the minor, resulting in a freedom from constraint that made for rapid advance. Miss M. H. Glyn, the authority mentioned above, explains succinctly the tonality of the virginalists as based on 'an inflectional scale, major in its rise, minor in its fall.' It is obvious that so elastic a tonal system brings in its train a vast range of subtly contrasting effects, accentuated by the impact of a new and still very simple harmonic

[1] There was another influence also tending to standardize the scale: the constant use of the hexachord, *ut*, *re*, *mi*, *fa*, *sol*, *la*, with its major third and perfect fourth.

scheme upon the intricate and flexible melodic one, developing on these inflectional lines. The clash of the horizontal against the vertical system necessitated perfectly logical 'false relations', bold discords and progressions apparently conflicting to the unaccustomed modern ear. The following examples are characteristic:

The resulting effects of colour, once the ear is attuned to them, constitute one of the charms of this early keyboard music and are more striking, though harsher, than similar effects in purely polyphonic vocal composition, where chromatic alteration of notes, in accordance with the rules of *musica ficta*, often produced the same result in complex part-writing.[1] In virginalistic technique the composer enjoyed a latitude hitherto unknown —the freedom of modality and the freedom of tonality and the limitations of neither. Out of this freedom was to emerge the rigidity of our major and minor scales, with its arbitrary rules of concord and discord.

It was much later that a clearly defined theory of tonality came into being, and the notation of virginal music, feeling its way to the new system, is involved in a riot of accidentals, while still using the one or two flat signatures of the old transposed or doubly transposed modes.

Notation

The prevailing fashion of written music, shown at its best in the notation of *My Ladye Nevells Booke*, abounds in evidence of the transitional nature of the period. The old convention of *musica ficta*,[2] implying accidentals where none were written in the text, survived in an unsystematic and inexact use of them in the notation of virginal music, based no longer on the modes but on the 'inflectional scale'. On a rapidly shifting system rules for the inclusion of accidentals in certain passages cannot be defined, nor

[1]The *sung* effect of such 'false relations' is, of course, softer than is possible on a keyed instrument like the virginal, which must have been tuned on some system of equal temperament. The effect in polyphony resulted from a sharpened leading note rising to the tonic in one part, written against a flattened leading note in another, falling to the fifth.

[2]*Musica ficta*, the chromatic alteration of notes in accordance with certain fixed rules based on natural laws of concord and discord.

the theory of procedure exactly ascertained. In *My Ladye Nevells Booke* the accidental, as a rule, alters only the note before which it is placed, the bar-line not having its modern significance. But this rule seems to be but casually observed, and even more so in other MSS. Undoubtedly, accidentals are often intended, though not written. A careful collation of one MS. with another frequently suggests a solution of doubtful points, but even then the unreliability of many texts makes it no positive proof; in a later version of an early MS. the custom of 'editing' on the part of the copyist, and the tendency later on to increase the number of sharpened leading notes, sometimes makes it impossible to discover exactly the composer's intention; the editor's difficulties are proportionately increased. The evidence supplied by lute versions of virginal pieces would solve many problems, but, unfortunately, very little keyboard music exists in lute tablature. In lute notation, of course, each note has its definite pitch, and no doubtful points arise as to *musica ficta* alterations.

The modern sign, ♮, for the natural is never found. A sharp—the old B quadratum—contradicted a flat—the B rotundum—and vice versa, but such restoration of chromatically altered notes was always unsystematic; on very rare occasions the sign ♮, found also in the Mulliner MS., is used for the natural in *My Ladye Nevells Booke.* Accidentals are placed above, below, or in front of a note.

Time-signatures in the modern sense as indications of rhythm were still non-existent; the old symbols of the greater and lesser prolation, ϕ, ϵ$_{3}$ and ¢, survive with a changing significance. The old mathematical system of 'proportions' was elaborate enough to indicate any possible combinations of time in intricate polyphony, but during the sixteenth century many of the symbols fell into disuse. Of the three surviving in the Nevell MS., ϕ$_{3}$ and ϵ originally signified the 'greater prolation', i.e. the proportion of three minims to the semibreve, ¢ the 'lesser prolation' with two minims to the semibreve. In the early vocal music they were purely arithmetical signs to guide the singer in unbarred part-writing. Such indications became unnecessary in scored and barred music, where part was written against part, and the barring, however irregular, fulfilled the same purpose. In much of the early scored keyboard music,[1] therefore, the signature is altogether dropped. In this later work, dating from *My Ladye Nevells Booke,* the obsolete symbols creep back with a hint of their modern indi-

[1] *Vide* the *Mulliner Book.*

cation of regular rhythm, Φ3 or C being found before pieces in simple triple time in minims, and ₵ before pieces in duple time, whether simple or compound. The old differentiation between square and round time by means of black and red notation survives in the black 'tripla'[1] of virginal music, used only in compound time, and always written in black semibreves and minims, and occasionally in black breves,[2] with the sign 31 whenever it occurs. This black tripla definitely denoted rhythmic change, though the sign 31 accompanying it was an arithmetical indication of diminution, i.e. the proportion of three black minims to one white one for the duration of the tripla section.

The introduction of regular accent into written music marked an epoch in the art, from which we may date the birth of modern notation; we find the convention of barring used for the first time in its modern sense, subject to lapses certainly, but following the natural regularity of accent in folk-song variations and rhythmic dance forms. The halving of the length of the bar is of common occurrence in florid repetitions and quickly moving semiquaver variations, following slow sections in semibreves and minims.

In contrapuntal forms like the fantasia, which follow the old flexible vocal line with constantly changing rhythm, the bar-line is still of no rhythmic significance whatever. There are countless instances in virginal music where barring is literally impossible as an indication of rhythm. It is the breaking of apparent regularity of accent by a sudden quickly passing rhythmic change that the growing use of regular bar-lines tended to obscure. The subtlety of rhythm within rhythm is, of course, a recognized point in editions of polyphonic music, and editorial bar-lines are only accepted as a compromise to facilitate reading, but in virginal pieces where the barring in the MS. follows the modern custom, the reader's half-unconscious reliance on it may lead to the obliteration of passing rhythmic fluctuations. Such a change as the following, from 3-2 time to 6-4, is constantly found (p. 115):

[1] *Vide* facsimile. [2] *Vide* facsimile.

The polyphonic habit of mind persists in the custom of writing as if in distinct parts, even when the structure is purely harmonic. The written effect is unwieldy and involved. The free style of part-writing for the virginal in the fantasia form gives the impression of a confused and muddled polyphony. With the adaptation of contrapuntal styles for the virginal, strict writing in three or four parts of fixed limits of range was replaced by a free counterpoint in which supernumerary parts entered at will and were lost in the general scheme, crossing, overlapping, two parts merging into one and disappearing with a constantly changing range of colour. Counterpoint at the outset in four parts was rarely in texture of more than three, though in range it would extend through four or five. The whole effect for the modern reader is one of careless writing, since any part entered without warning, and its absence was rarely, and even then unsystematically, indicated by rests.[1]

The F, G, and C clefs were used on almost any line of the six-lined stave to avoid leger lines, the clefs moving up and down the stave in the course of a piece as the pitch varied.

There are numerous indications of the fingering of virginal music in the text of *My Ladye Nevells Booke*. It seems to have been a crude system, developed later on the lines of our modern one. The fingers are evidently numbered 12345 in the right hand and the reverse in the left hand, the thumb being 5 and the little finger 1. The same method is used in the *Fitzwilliam Book* MS.

Virginal music was overburdened with ornaments, both as written-out shakes and trills and further indicated by signs,  and less frequently,  . The effect on the virginal was undoubtedly brilliant, and florid ornament of this type was a specifically virginalistic development. Comparison of texts reveals the fact that the sign  in one is often written out in full in another. There is adequate evidence of the sort from fairly closely related texts to indicate that  should be interpreted as a shake,  , or  . The other sign,  , is much more rarely encountered. There is not sufficient evidence of the same sort to solve the problem. In one instance the comparison of two texts seems to imply that it should be

[1] *Vide* facsimile.

interpreted as a slide. But similar evidence in another place implies a mordent, [musical notation], and this is perhaps a more probable solution. Such shakes and trills when written-out appear in quavers, semiquavers, or demi-semiquavers indiscriminately: there is no attempt at accurate grouping. In performance on a modern piano they are better left out: they destroy the melodic line and burden the structure of the piece with unnecessary elaboration, while increasing the technical difficulties for the performer.

It must be remembered that the character of the virginal was totally different from the modern pianoforte. The sixteenth-century virginal was a much smaller and slighter instrument than the harpsichord, which developed later from it: the tone—obtained by the plucked string, distinct from the struck string of the early clavichord and the modern pianoforte—was clear, slight, and sweet. Sustained tone and *legato* as we know it on the modern pianoforte was impossible. On the other hand, rapid passages and florid ornaments, shakes and trills were all brilliant and very effective in a characteristic way that we cannot imitate on the piano. It is through this inability to reproduce it exactly that the superficial effectiveness of much virginal music is lost for us, or a wrong impression of it gained. Much of this florid figuration is better omitted altogether.

The question of equal temperament of the virginal was raised on a previous page in the discussion of 'false relations'. It cannot be disputed that some such system was in use for keyed instruments in Byrd's time, if not before. There is sufficient evidence of this in the use of D♯ and E♭,[1] and of G♯ and A♭ in virginal music, and even in the same piece, implying a system of tuning in which D♯ and E♭ were identical, and G♯ and A♭. In just temperament this would, of course, not be the case. The conclusion to be drawn is that some system of dividing the scale into twelve equal semitones must have been used.

Editorial Method

The system adopted in the present critical edition is an attempt to obliterate as little as possible peculiarities of notation in the MS. which it is desirable to reproduce for the student of Tudor technique, and at the same time to present to the average reader and performer a clear modern text, burdened neither with archaic conventions nor with an individual

[1] In the note to No. 9 (p. xl, *q.v.*) there is further reference to this point.

editorial reading. The method is necessarily a compromise. An examination of the facsimiles will make clear the main differences between the old obsolete system of notation and the modern one. The problem of *musica ficta* is the editor's chief concern: a problem presented in the foregoing account of virginal notation, and which only a study of contemporary virginal music and of the principles of sixteenth-century virginalistic technique can help to solve. Such principles bearing on the question of *musica ficta* have already been discussed.[1]

In the present edition the convention adhered to is as follows, it being assumed that accidentals in the MS. affect only the notes next to which they are actually placed, and do not persist through the bar as in modern notation.

All accidentals in the MS. text are reproduced in their ordinary position, except (*a*) redundant accidentals within the same bar, which are omitted in accordance with modern practice, and (*b*) obvious copyist's mistakes, also omitted in this edition with a footnote reference. It will be noted that the frequent though unsystematic MS. 'cautionary accidentals', restoring a previously altered note to its original pitch, but outside the bar in which the original alteration occurs, are, though also redundant, reproduced in this text. Accidentals not in the MS., but added by the editor, are always placed above or below the notes to be altered; where an accidental is placed before a note the first time it occurs in a bar, but not subsequently in the same bar, though obviously intended, the necessary accidental is placed as an editorial addition above the notes to be altered; only by this means can the original MS. reading be made exactly clear. For example, [music example] in the MS. is reproduced as [music example] in this edition. Such unsystematic use of accidentals in the MS. is of common occurrence.

Modern time-signatures are not put in—the barring, where regular, indicates whether the time is duple or triple; and where the barring is irregular, a time-signature would be equally useless and misleading. The old symbols have been left in their original positions in the MS. The black 'tripla', occurring throughout a piece as in the 'Carmans Whistle' or the 'Woods soe Wylde', is transcribed in modern 6-4 time, the unit of time in the bar, the dotted minim, being unaltered all through. But tripla occurring in the

[1] *Supra*, pp. xxviii, xxix.

course of a piece, written as counterpoint against white minims, and always indicating the change of rhythm in the tripla part from 2-2 to 6-4, or from 3-2 to 9-4, is indicated by triplet crotchets in this edition; it has been considered preferable to adopt the convention of triplets against the minim rather than to change the minim to the dotted minim, which gives the misleading impression of a bar lengthened from one of two or three minims to that of two or three dotted minims; it should be clear that the minim unit of time in the bar persists throughout the tripla section with the quickened pace of the tripla against it.

The MS. barring is left unaltered in this edition, except for occasional instances of obvious slips, when footnote reference is made. Dotted bar-lines, implying editorial additions, have also been added on the many occasions where clarity in the modern text demands it, where MS. bars are unduly long, or single bar-lines used in the MS. instead of double ones to mark variation endings. The ornamented double bar of the MS. is replaced by a plain double bar.

The use of tied notes in the MS. is comparatively infrequent; in this edition both the dotted and tied notes are retained exactly as they stand in the MS., except (*a*) at bar-endings, where a note tied over to the next bar is substituted for a dotted note, e.g.  for  and (*b*) in intricate semiquaver passages where the use of the tie much simplifies reading.[1] Any other exceptional cases are referred to footnotes. Although in many cases the notation would be clearer if a definite convention in the use of tied notes were observed, in this edition it has been considered more important to reproduce, even at this sacrifice of a certain degree of clarity, the unsystematic procedure in the MS. showing the rhythmic freedom within the bar. The constant use of tied notes produces a misleading effect of syncopation.

The modern use of F and G clefs only in their usual position on five-lined staves is, of course, substituted for the more elaborate clef system of the MS. The MS. practice is apparently to set all notes for the right hand on the upper stave and for the left hand on the lower, but the use of two clefs only in fixed position in the modern edition makes it essential occasionally to move notes from one stave to the other to avoid the clumsy effect of leger lines. Quavers and semiquavers in the MS., written

[1] The last six bars on p. 76 are also simplified in this way.

often with separate tails, are here systematically grouped. All editorial alterations are referred to footnotes, except in the case of the innumerable shakes and trills indiscriminately written in quavers, semiquavers, or demisemiquavers in the MS., and here correctly grouped and altered to the modern system without comment. The movement of parts from one stave to another is indicated in obscure passages. Editorial additions of bracketed rests to make the absence or entry of parts clearer in contrapuntal writing are as few as possible, the MS. practice being reproduced except where passages are unusually involved. The unsystematic MS. use of breve or semibreve rests for whole bars of varying length is also reproduced. It is impossible, without entirely destroying the character of the original MS., to reduce the eccentricities of notation to a strictly systematic text. Repeated sections are marked off by dotted double bar-lines, and the erratic numbering of variations and fingering indications are left as they stand in the MS.

Footnote reference is occasionally made to other MS. readings.

MS. SOURCES CONSULTED[1]

Other MS. versions of many pieces in *My Ladye Nevells Booke* exist; these MS. sources are given below. Exact references will be found in the detailed notes on each piece.

The *Fitzwilliam Virginal Book* (now edited and published).
The *Will Forster Book* (in the Royal Library, on permanent loan to the British Museum).
The *Elizabeth Rogers Virginal Book*, British Museum Additional MS. 10337.
British Museum Add. MS. 30485. (*Extracts from Lady Nevil's Book.*)
British Museum Add. MS. 30486.
British Museum Add. MS. 31392.
British Museum Add. MS. 31403.
Christ Church Library, Oxford, MS. 431.
Paris Conservatoire Library MS. 18546.
Paris Conservatoire Library MS. 18547. (Autograph MS. of Thomas Tomkins.)
New York Public Library, Drexel MS. 5612.

British Museum Egerton MS. 2046 contains a lute version of No. 33 in the Nevell MS., and British Museum Add. MS. 17786-89, 17791 a string version of No. 29.

With these MS. sources may be included the early printed book *Parthenia* (1611).

MODERN EDITIONS OF VIRGINAL MUSIC BY BYRD[2]

Nos. 1, 2, 4, 6, 7, 17-21, 23, 26, 29, 30, 41 and 42 in *My Ladye Nevells Booke* have not been published hitherto in any version. Of these, Nos. 1, 6, 7, 23, 26, 30 and 42 are peculiar to the Nevell MS. Versions of Nos. 3, 8-15, 22, 24, 25, 27, 28, 31-38 are in the *Fitzwilliam Virginal Book*, edited by J. A. Fuller-Maitland and W. Barclay Squire (Breitkopf und Härtel); of No. 3 in the same editors' *Selected Pieces from the Fitzwilliam Virginal Book* (Chester); of Nos. 12, 13, and 33 in *Fourteen Selected Pieces,* also edited by Fuller-Maitland and Squire (Stainer and Bell); of Nos. 5, 13, 14, 15, 16 (abridged), 22 (abridged), 31 (abridged), 35 (abridged), 39 and 40 in Margaret H. Glyn's popular edition, *The Byrd Organ Book* (W. Reeves); of Nos. 39 and 40 in the same editor's popular edition of *Parthenia* (W. Reeves); of the Irishe Marche from No. 4 in the same editor's *Dances Grave and Gay* (Winthrop Rogers); of Nos. 27, 33 and 34 in Granville Bantock's popular edition, *Selected Pieces* (Novello); of Nos. 5, 34 and 37 in Vol. I of *The Golden Treasury of Music*, popularly edited by Oesterle (Schirmer); and of

[1] This list is limited to MSS. containing versions of Nevell pieces. The remaining MS. sources of Byrd's virginal music are the *Cosyn Book*, in the Royal Library, and Ch.Ch. MSS. 1175, 371, and 1113, each including one piece only by Byrd.

[2] This list is limited to editions containing versions of Nevell pieces. The only other sources are Fuller-Maitland and Squire's *Selected Pieces from Cosyn's Book* (Chester), and T. F. Dunhill's *Old English Dances,* Vol. I (J. Williams).

Nos. 5, 34, 39 and 40 in Vol. II of Farrenc's *Trésor des Pianistes*, a mid-nineteenth-century edition of doubtful accuracy. (It was this Mme. Farrenc to whom Rimbault lent various virginal MSS., and who originally owned the English virginal MSS. now in the Library at the Conservatoire de Musique in Paris.)

Rimbault's *Parthenia* and other popular editions of manifest inaccuracy are not included in this list.

BIBLIOGRAPHY

Among modern publications the following will be found particularly useful to the student of virginal music and of the rise of keyboard technique:

Henry Davey: *History of English Music* (Curwen, 1921).

Charles van den Borren: *Sources of Keyboard Music in England* (Novello, 1914).

Margaret H. Glyn: *English Virginal Music and Composers* (W. Reeves, 1924).

There are also the usual sources of information in standard reference books, and the valuable untranslated works on the subject by the German scholars, Nagel, Ambros, and Seiffert. André Pirro's *Les Clavécinistes* (1924) is a valuable modern appreciation.

ANALYTICAL NOTES

(The foliation in the Nevell MS. is given after the number of each piece; British Museum Additional MSS. are abbreviated to Add.; references are to the modern edition of the Fitzwilliam MS.)

1\. f. 1. Found only in Nevell MS. This piece and Nos. 2 and 26 were evidently written specially for Lady Nevell. It consists of six variations on a very simple ground twenty-four bars in length, forming a strict harmonic basis, though not a strict bass; and in the last three variations the bass is at times quite free and the harmony sustained in the upper parts. Considerable interest is given to the fourth variation by the use of cross rhythms moving from part to part, a 6-4 rhythm in one part against 3-2 in another. The figuration is comparatively simple.

2\. f. 8. In *Forster*, p. 63, as 'Kapassa.' Apparently a dance form in round time, here in three sections, each forty three-minim bars long, related by practically the same harmonic basis. It is in effect three variations on an irregular ground. In Add. 29485 f. 5 is an anonymous piece called 'Galliard Quy passe' and, in a later hand, 'for my Lady Nevill', but it has no connection with this Nevell piece.

3\. f. 13b. In *Fitzwilliam Book*, Vol. II, p. 402, as 'The Earl of Oxford's March.' It is not found in the other MS. versions of the Battell piece.

4\. f. 19. In Ch.Ch. MS. 431; Paris MS. 18546. f. 93b; Add. 10337. f. 11b. These versions are all later, and vary in detail from the Nevell text; the Ch.Ch. MS. is incomplete and obviously the work of a careless scribe.

This naive attempt at battle music, though technically very trivial, is not without interest as one of the earliest known programme pieces; the trumpet, bagpipe and drone, and flute and drum sections are all efforts at realistic imitation of an elementary type. The version in Add. 10337 has a concluding section not found in the Nevell MS. called 'The Buriing of the Dead'; this short fragment is almost identical with another piece, the fifth section from the Medley by Byrd in the *Fitzwilliam Book*, where it is written a fourth higher; there seems to be some connection between this Medley and the Battell music, since the preceding section in the Medley bears a strong resemblance to the trumpet section in the Battell piece. 'The Buriing of the Dead' is included in the present edition, together with two other short sections not found in the Nevell text, the 'Morris' and the 'Souldiers Dance', taken from Paris MS. 18546, where they are interpolated between the 'March to the Fight' and the 'Retreate'. These three sections must be later additions to the Battell music, since both sources are considerably later than the Nevell MS., where the piece is apparently complete without them. Neither the Ch.Ch. MS. nor Add. 10337 contains 'The Galliarde for the Victorie', which follows.

5\. f. 32. In Paris MS. 18546 f. 114b. as 'Victoria.' It is constructed on the usual galliard plan.

6\. f. 34. Found only in Nevell MS. The barlye-breake was a country game and dance which could be accompanied by some sort of musical medley. The piece is in thirteen unrelated sections, each having its repeat, and of varying lengths, some breaking into a 'tripla' movement. The first, third and fourth sections are given in a mutilated version in Chappell's *Old English Popular Music*, Vol. I (p. 70), as a folk-dance tune. Technically, the piece is characteristic of Byrd's most vigorous work, and in some passages, notably the fourth section (p. 45), the harmonic effects are of variety and beauty.

7. f. 43. Found only in Nevell MS. This very simple dance falls into two distinct main sections (bars 1-32 and bars 32 to the end), of which the second is a variation of the first; each section is again subdivided into four four-bar phrases, on an unusual scheme, A, B, C, B1, each with a repeat; the construction of the entire piece may therefore be tabulated:

First section	A	A1	repeat	A2	A3
	B	B1		B4	B5
	C	C1		C2	C3
	B2	B3		B6	B7

8. f. 46. In the *Fitzwilliam Book* as 'Pescodd Time', Vol. II, p. 430, and as 'The Hunts Up', Vol. I, p. 218, where the version differs considerably, both in detail and in order of variations, of which there are twelve. It is constructed as variations on a ground. The harmonic basis remains the same throughout, though at times the bass moves freely in florid counterpoint.

It has no apparent connection with 'The Hunts Up' tune, found in Chappell's *Old English Popular Music,* Vol. I, p. 86, afterwards also known as 'Peascod Time'. The generic title of 'hunt's up' was given to any 'morning song' or 'morning music', a title derived apparently from the words sung to the original tune, of which the first verse is as follows:

'The hunt is up, the hunt is up,
And it is well nigh day;
And Harry our King has gone hunting
To bring his deer to bay.'

9. f. 52b. In *Fitzwilliam Book*, Vol. I, p. 395. The six notes of the hexachord, ascending and descending, were a favourite basis for variations. These of Byrd's are simple compared with the harmonic intricacies of Bull's hexachord fantasia in the *Fitzwilliam Book*,[1] one of the most remarkable pieces of the period. Mention has been made before[2] of Byrd's piece of the same type in Paris MS. 18547, where Tomkins' note in the MS. calls it 'a good lesson of Mr. Byrdes the playne song briefes to be played by a second person.' In this Nevell piece, Byrd uses only the hexachords starting on C, G, D, F, and B♭, involving none of the advanced enharmonic changes found in Bull's variations, where the hexachord is used on every note of the scale, rising with each fresh variation by a whole tone, i.e. on G, A, B, D♭, E♭, F, then on by a minor third to A♭, B♭, C, D, E, F♯, and finally to G again. Bull's piece is unique in virginal music, and must be cited here as a comparative case, of which the chief interest is that the use of D♭ and C♯, E♭ and D♯, A♭ and G♯, in the same piece, proves conclusively the theory that a system of equal temperament was in use for keyed instruments. Byrd's variations here are comparatively simple. The use of rhythmic folk-song-like figures as a contrapuntal device in imitation is exemplified on pp. 70, 73.

10. f. 58b. In *Fitzwilliam Book*, Vol. II, p. 204, where there is a note in the margin of the MS., 'the first t(hat) ever hee m(ade)'. The binding has obliterated the letters in brackets. This and the following eight pavans and galliards are all constructed on the usual three-strain plan.

11. f. 61b. In *Fitzwilliam Book*, Vol. II, p. 207.

[1] *Fitzwilliam Book*, Vol. I, p. 183.
[2] *Supra,* p. xxvii.

12. f. 63. In *Fitzwilliam Book*, Vol. II, p. 398, as 'Pavan Fant[asia]'; *Forster*, p. 114; Add. 30485 f. 6b.

13. f. 65. In *Fitzwilliam Book*, Vol. II, p. 400; *Forster*, p. 240; Add. 30485 f. 7. In *Forster* it is unrelated to the pavan, occurring much later in the MS. and called 'Mr. Birds Galliard.'

14. f. 67. In *Fitzwilliam Book*, Vol. II, p. 384; Add. 30485 f. 4; Add. 31392 f. 1; Drexel 5612, No. 54.

15. f. 69b. In *Fitzwilliam Book*, Vol. II, p. 387; Add. 30485 f. 5b; Add. 31392 f. 2b; Drexel 5612, No. 55. The long bars are left as they are in the MS. in order not to hide the shifting rhythms within the bar, constantly changing from 3-2 to 6-4.

16. f. 71b. In Add. 30485 f. 81.

17. f. 73b. In Add. 30485 f. 82b.

18. f. 75 b. In Add. 31392 f. 3b; Drexel 5612, No. 96.

19. f. 78b. In Add. 31392 f. 5b; Drexel 5612, No. 97.

20. f. 80b. In Add. 31392 f. 9b; Add. 30485 f. 105b. The third strain and its repeat are remarkable for unusually modern effects of modulation.

21. f. 84. In Add. 31392 f. 11b; Add. 30485 f. 107.

22. f. 86. In *Fitzwilliam Book*, Vol. II, p. 427, called 'Canon: two parts in one.' The canon, between the two upper parts, is strict and easy to follow, except in the repeats, where it is lost in the florid figuration. In spite of its academic form, this pavan is constructed on the usual plan of three strains each with a repeat. It has no galliard following it.

23. f. 89. Found only in the Nevell MS. This again has no galliard.

24. f. 92. In *Fitzwilliam Book*, Vol. I, p. 203; *Forster*, p. 217; Add. 30486 f. 7. 'The Passamezzo', or 'Passing mesures pavan', was different in form from the ordinary three-strain pavan, being constructed upon one strain followed by variations. The strain is sixteen two-semibreve bars in length, and followed by five variations; the Fitzwilliam version has six variations. It was evidently a slow dance in square time, followed by a quicker measure in round time, corresponding, though not in form, to the ordinary pavan and galliard.

25. f. 99b. In *Fitzwilliam Book*, Vol. I, p. 209, omitting fifth section; *Forster*, p. 230; Add. 30486 f. 11. This galliard is closely related to the foregoing pavan both thematically and harmonically. In form it is constructed on the same basis of one sixteen-bar strain followed by variations, of which there are nine. In the MS. there is an E♭ in the signature of the galliard, but not in that of the pavan. This must be a copyist's mistake, since the close relation between pavan and galliard makes it unlikely such a difference would occur. The prevailing tonality throughout both is that of G, and all the strains close on the chord of G. E♭ occurs frequently in both pieces as an accidental, and in the galliard such additions would be redundant if the E♭ in the signature were intentional. These and the constant MS. correcting accidentals make the exact reading fairly clear in spite of the doubtful signature. It is possible that the E♭ was put in with the original object of convenience for the scribe, to avoid the use of accidentals in the course of the piece. It is omitted in the last two sections.

26. f. 105b. Found only in Nevell MS. An introductory section of seven bars is followed by a free development of several subjects one after the other, the subjects degenerating towards the end into constantly changing imitated figures.

27. f. 109. In *Fitzwilliam Book*, Vol. I, p. 263; *Forster*, p. 118; Add. 30485 f. 67; Add. 31403 f. 23b; the first two variations are also found in Paris MS. 18546 f. 17. In the Nevell MS. and Add. 30485 it is dated 1590. It consists of twelve variations upon the tune, unsystematically numbered in the MS., and the theme as always has no original simple statement. The construction is half harmonic, on a bass alternating between F and G, and half contrapuntal with a freely moving bass; the tune does not persist strictly throughout, being in some of the variations lost in the florid figuration; it moves freely from part to part. Mention has already been made[1] of another use of this tune by Byrd as a contrapuntal variation on the hexachord. According to Chappell[2], the original words to the melody, evidently a popular one, have been lost.

28. f. 113. In *Fitzwilliam Book*, Vol. II, p. 67. A set of eight contrapuntal variations on 'The Maidens Song' theme, which appears mainly in the uppermost part. The figuration is elaborate.

29. f. 119b. In Paris MS. 18547, p. 19, called 'Mr. Birdes Fantasy: two parts in one.' In Add. 17786-89, 17791 as a five-part string piece with which the Paris MS. short score is identical. This version differs considerably from that in the Nevell MS. An interesting point arises, since it is evident that the Nevell version, though purely contrapuntal, is not a short score of this later MS. string piece. There is nothing in the piece to indicate that it was specially written for the virginal and, indeed, everything to indicate that it was not, since it contains no virginalistic figuration whatever, but if adapted from a string piece it must have been an earlier and very different version from that of Add. 17786-89, 17791. Such adaptations were of common occurrence. The three famous six-part string fantasias of Byrd's are to be found as keyboard pieces in Add. 29996. But the early contrapuntal string idiom loses half its interest when played on a keyed instrument. This piece is interesting for the figures used in imitation on pp. 159, 160, obviously of folk-tune derivation.

30. f. 126. Found only in Nevell MS. There are here, excluding the original varied statement, sixteen variations on a ground (numbered in the MS. from the fourth). The ground is twelve three-minim bars in length, and appears as a fairly strict bass upon which the first eleven variations are built up; in each of the remaining six the theme, divided into four phrases, appears with altered harmonies alternately in the uppermost part and the bass. The piece is full of technical interest, though harmonic effects are often harsh and crude. It is longer and rather more elaborate than the other ground variations in the MS.

31. f. 135. In *Fitzwilliam Book*, Vol. I, p. 267; *Forster*, p. 74; Add. 30486 f. 2. According to Chappell[3], 'Walsingham' is an old folk-tune dating from pre-Reformation times. The verses to the tune begin:

> 'As I went to Walsingham,
> To the shrine with speed,
> Met I with a jolly palmer
> In a pilgrim's weed.'

This gives the date of their origin before the suppression of pilgrimages; the Priory of Walsingham was a famous shrine. These twenty-two variations on the tune, followed

[1] *Supra*, p. xxvii.
[2] *Old English Popular Music*, Vol. I, p. 119.
[3] *Ibid.*, Vol. I, p. 69.

by a short final section, are elaborate and purely contrapuntal; the theme moves freely among the parts.

32. f. 142b. In *Fitzwilliam Book*, Vol. I, p. 411. The tune is incorrectly set to 6-4 time by Chappell.[1] The 6-4 compound duple rhythm was invariably written in black tripla notation, a definite rhythmic indication; duplicity of rhythm in every instance in the Nevell MS. is indicated by ¢. This piece is preceded by Є, never set before compound duple rhythm, and written in white notes. It must be remembered that, though the sign was a survival of an outworn system, there is a recognizable connection between modern 3-2 time and the old significance of Є to divide the semibreve into three minims. One could trace no possible sequence of method in setting Є before a piece in which duplicity of time division occurred. The possibility of a copyist's mistake in setting Є instead of ¢ in the Nevell version is removed by the accompanying evidence of white note notation. The harmonic basis of all six variations is practically the same. The melody appears in the uppermost part in all but the last, where it moves down to the alto. There seem to be no known words to this tune. The original song was sung to another in 2-4 time.

33. f. 145b. In *Fitzwilliam Book*, Vol. II, p. 180, there called 'Rowland'; *Forster*, p. 22; Paris MS. 18586 f. 64b, with one flat only in signature; Egerton 2046 f. 33b, in lute tablature. The Forster MS. omits bars 13-23; the Paris MS. omits the middle section. The piece falls into three sections, the first a statement of the tune, the last two free variations of it on the same harmonic basis as the first. The tune is here constructed on a phrase A repeated, followed by another phrase B, also repeated. According to Chappell,[2] who omits the repetition of the second half of the tune, the words sung to it are the following, from the Roxburghe Collection:

'The fifteenth day of July,
with glistering spear and shield
A famous fight in flanders
was foughten in the field;
The most couragious officers
was English Captains three;
But the bravest man in Battell
was brave Lord Willoughby.'

If this verse was originally sung to the tune, the repetition of phrase B was an extra variation, added by Byrd. Musically the melody is complete without it.

The tune is found in a slightly different version without the E♭ in one of the early Dutch printed collections, Adriaen Valerius's *Nederlandtsche Gedenck-Clank* (1626), p. 83, under the name 'Soet Robbert.' This is evidently a confusion of titles with the folk-tune, 'Bonny Sweet Robin'. Several other English tunes are found in the book, and it is not extraordinary that such a mistake should arise in a foreign collection, where names and tunes were unfamiliar to the collector.

34. f. 149. In *Fitzwilliam Book*, Vol. I, p. 214; *Forster*, p. 130, called a 'Ground'; Add. 30485 f. 65; Add. 30486 f. 19, with the final section omitted; Add. 31403 f. 25b. In the first eight of these nine variations the melody is in the uppermost part, moving to the alto for the last. The harmonic basis changes freely. The first variation is preceded by a four-bar introduction consisting of a simple statement of the first two bars of the tune in the

[1] *Old English Popular Music*, Vol. I, p. 81.
[2] *Ibid.*, Vol. I, p. 152.

alto alone, imitated a fifth below in the tenor; this four-bar phrase leads straight on without a break, making the first section sixteen bars in length instead of twelve. The original ballad sung to the tune was apparently of great length, and the tune itself of immense popularity.[1]

35. f. 153b. In *Fitzwilliam Book,* Vol. I, p. 226, as 'Treg(ians) Ground'; *Forster,* p. 390, called 'a Grounde'; Add. 30485 f. 61, called 'Mr Birds Ground.' All the variations but two are built up on a strict ground bass; in the sixth and eighth the bass moves freely, but the same harmonic basis persists.

Hugh Aston has been mentioned before as an important figure in the history of virginal music.[2] In Ch.Ch. MSS. 979-83[3] (f. 163) there is a string piece, 'Hugh Astons Maske', ascribed to Aston in the superius and sexta pars, and to Whytbrooke in the contratenor (tenor deest); the opening phrase of this piece bears a certain melodic resemblance to the Ground in the Nevell MS., but the vaguely defined thematic character of the latter makes it impossible to establish a definite connection between them.

36. f. 161. In *Fitzwilliam Book,* Vol. I, p. 37. The first section here is based on one subject worked out in vigorous counterpoint; it is followed by a homophonic second section leading on without a break to the usual rambling development of imitated figures and florid figuration.

37. f. 166. In *Fitzwilliam Book,* Vol. I, p. 248. The nine variations on the twenty-bar tune vary in type; the harmonic basis changes with a freely moving bass in some of the later sections. The melody, often lost in elaborate figuration, moves between the two upper parts. The tune was sometimes known as 'The Beginning of the World'[4]. It seems to have been one of the best-known and most popular melodies of the day, and many different verses and ballads were set to it. No original words are known.

38. f. 173b. In *Fitzwilliam Book,* Vol. I, p. 238, as 'Variatio' following another 'Monsieurs Alman'; *Forster,* p. 366; Add. 30485 f. 92b. For purposes of analysis the piece falls into three main sections, the last two variations of the first, which is subdivided into a sixteen-semibreve phrase A, repeated, followed by a phrase B of the same length, also repeated. The last two sections, therefore, consist of further variations of A and B, constructed on the same harmonic sequence. There is no defined melodic idea in either A or B for variation. The development is florid throughout.

39. f. 180b. In *Parthenia; Forster,* p. 311; Add. 30486 f. 14; Drexel 5612, No. 72. In *Parthenia* and the Drexel MS. the last five bars are condensed into three. Neither Add. 30486 nor the Drexel MS. contains the galliard.

40. f. 184b. In *Parthenia; Forster,* p. 74.

41. f. 186b. Add. 30485 f. 103b. The four-bar homophonic second section is an interesting example of flexible rhythm; the two halves of the section overlap, each phrase of ten minims forming a melodic curve in which definite accent at any point is impossible. The *fugato* development of the piece is of great variety and beauty, unmarred by the formless figuration developed in so many fantasias of the same type.

42. f. 191. Found only in Nevell MS.

[1] Chappell, *Old English Popular Music,* Vol. I, p. 253.
[2] *Supra,* p. xxiii.
[3] The *Baldwin Part-books* referred to earlier, p. xxi.
[4] Chappell, *Old English Popular Music,* Vol. I, p. 256.

MY LADYE NEVELLS BOOKE

I. MY LADYE NEVELS GROWNDE.

1) D not dotted in MS.

F♯

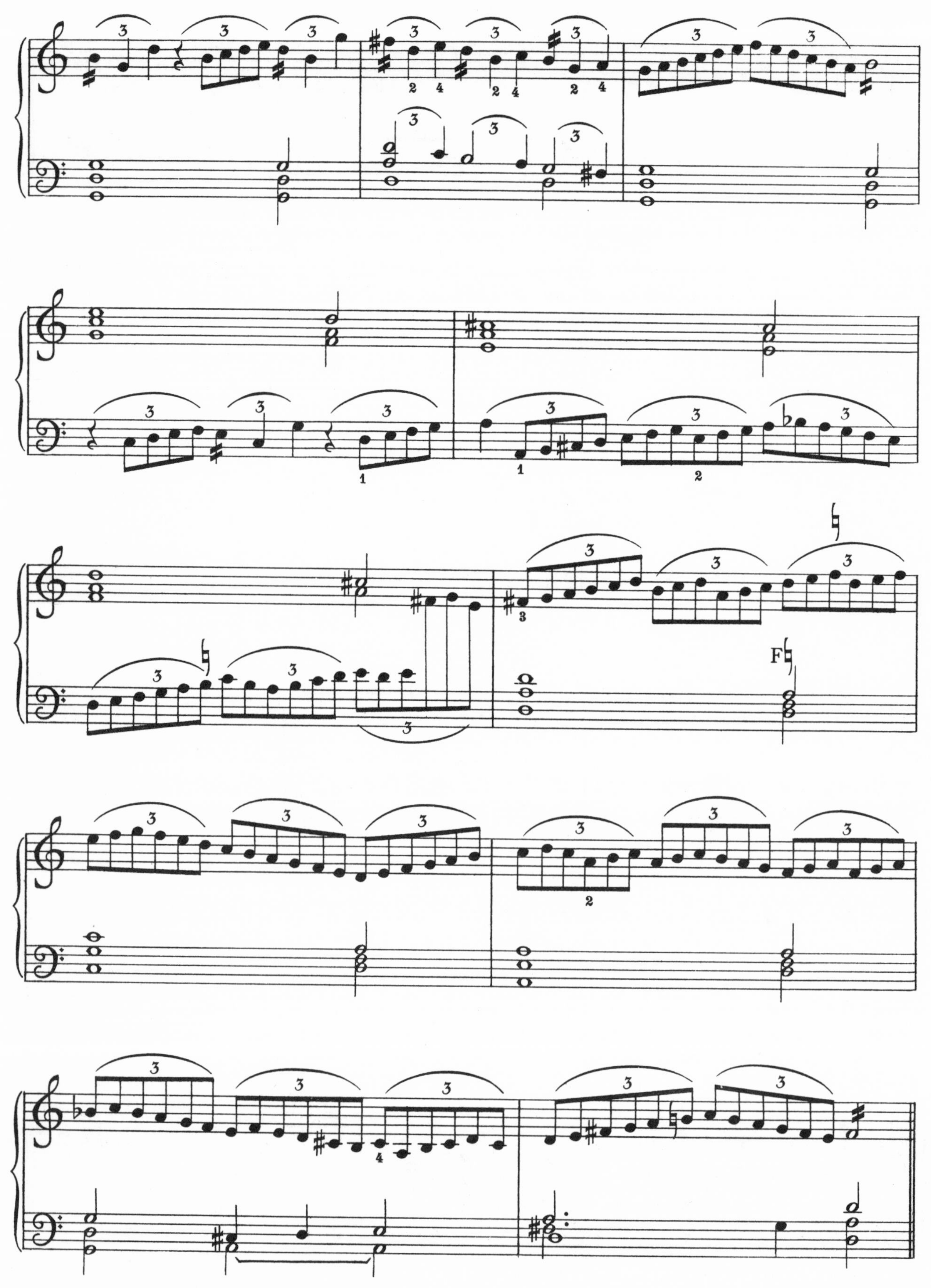

finis mr. w. birde.

2. QUI PASSE:
for my ladye nevell.

1) G instead of A in MS.

1) barline here in MS.

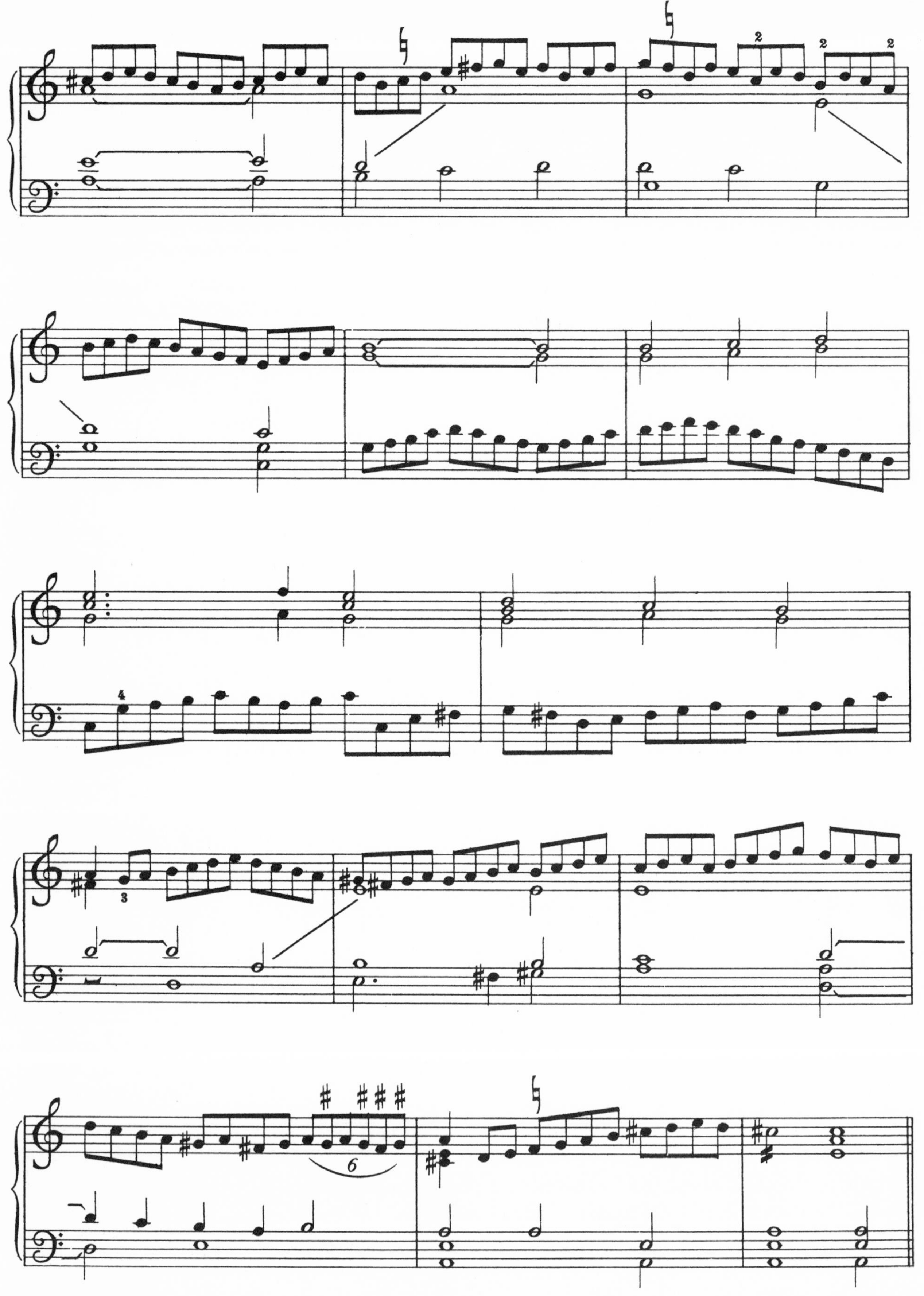

finis. mr. w. birde.

3. THE MARCHE BEFORE THE BATTELL.

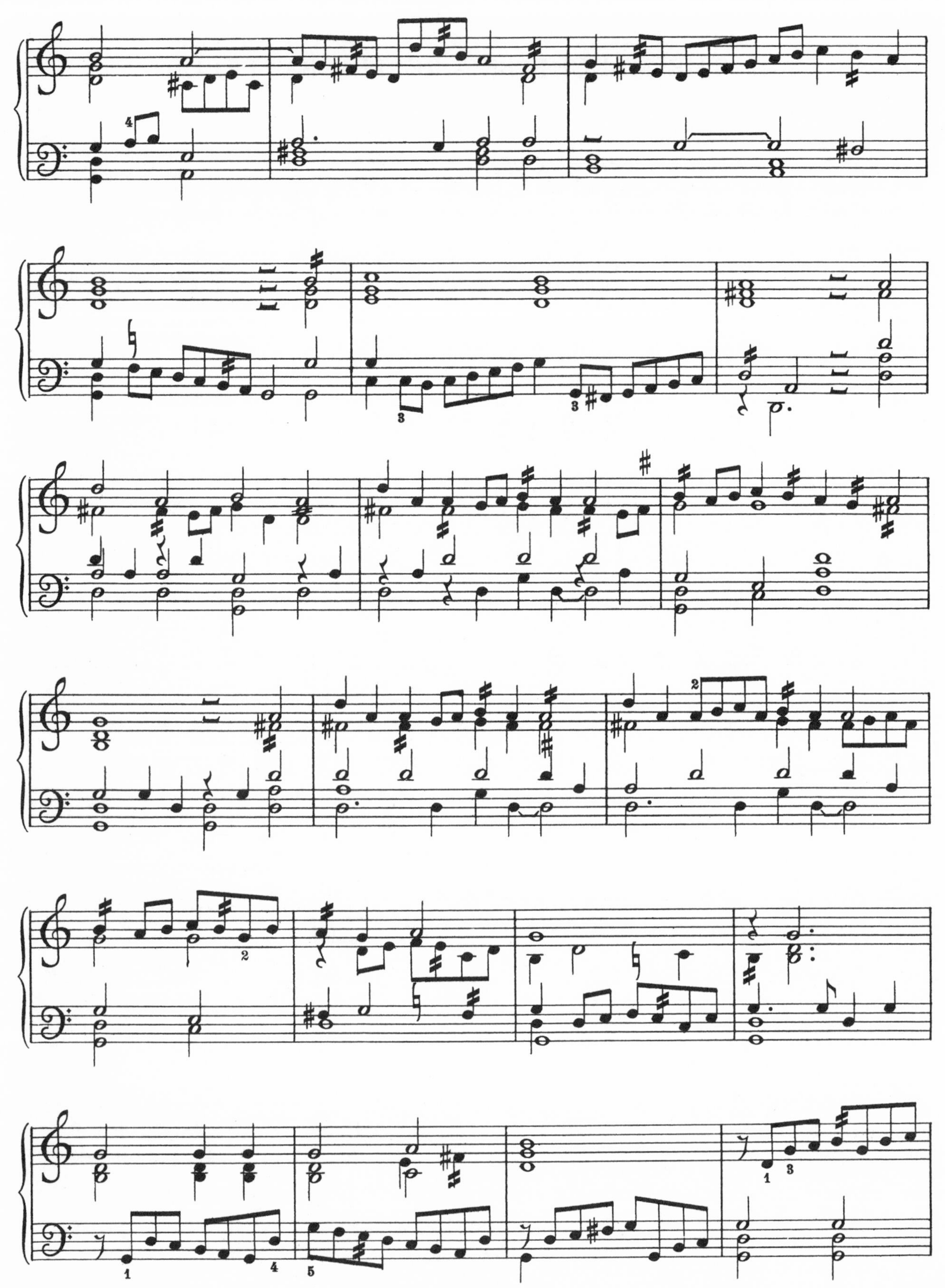

1) crotchet rest here in MS.

1) only six demisemiquavers in MS.

1) quavers in MS. 2) D♯ in MS. 3) G not tied in MS.

4. THE BATTELL.

1) the first C is a quaver in MS. the crotchet is supplied from Add. 10337. It is not tied in the MS. but obviously should be.

The marche of footemen.

The marche of horsmen.

now folowethe the trupetts:

The trumpetts.

The Irishe marche.

The bagpipe and the drone.

The flute and the droome.

1) barline here in MS.

6

The marche to the fighte.

1) A instead of G in MS.

tantara tantara

the battels be joyned:
3
6

The retreat.

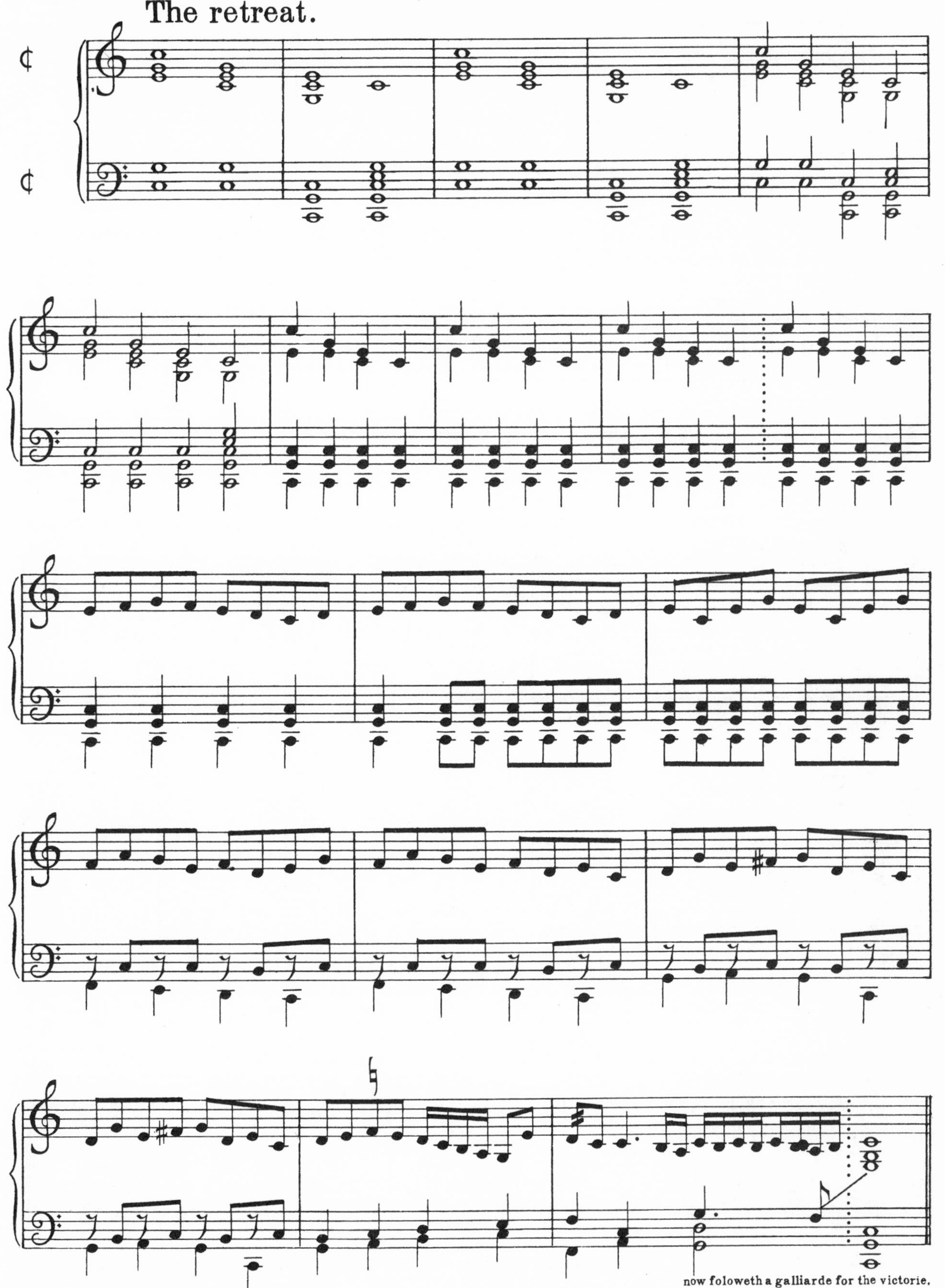
now foloweth a galliarde for the victorie.

From the Elizabeth Rogers Virginal Book (B.M. Add. MS. 10337.) [1)]

1) This section and the two immediately following are not in the Nevell text. They are interpolated here from two later versions of the Battel piece.

From Paris Conservatoire MS. 18546.

5. THE GALLIARDE FOR THE VICTORIE.

1) barline here in MS.

mr.w. birde.

6. THE BARELYE BREAKE.

F♯

1) G♯ in MS.

1) B indicated in MS. by direct.

1) G instead of A in MS.

1) G not dotted in MS.

mr. w. birde. gentleman of her maiesties chappell.

7. A GALLIARDS GYGGE.

1) barline here in MS.

mr. w. birde. organiste of her maiesties chappell.

8. THE HUNTES UPP.

1) barline here in MS.

1) barline here in MS.

1) E not in MS.

1) barline here in MS.

1) quavers in MS.

1) barline here in MS. 2) A semibreve in MS.

mr. w. birde: laus sit deo

9. UT RE MI FA SOL LA.

1) barline here in MS.

1) F instead of A in MS. 2) barline here in MS.

3
3
3
3

1) G in MS. It must obviously be E to complete the ascending hexachord.

1) E indicated by direct in MS.

10. THE FIRSTE PAVIAN.

1) no time signature in MS. 2) barline here in MS. 3) not tied in MS.

1) C♯ in MS.

1) minim rest in MS. 2) C not in MS.

finis:the galliarde foloweth.

II. THE GALLIARDE TO THE FIRSTE PAVIAN.

finis: mr. w. birde.

12. THE SECONDE PAVIAN.

1) crotchet rest here in MS.   2) B not in MS; supplied from Add. 30485.

1) D not in MS.

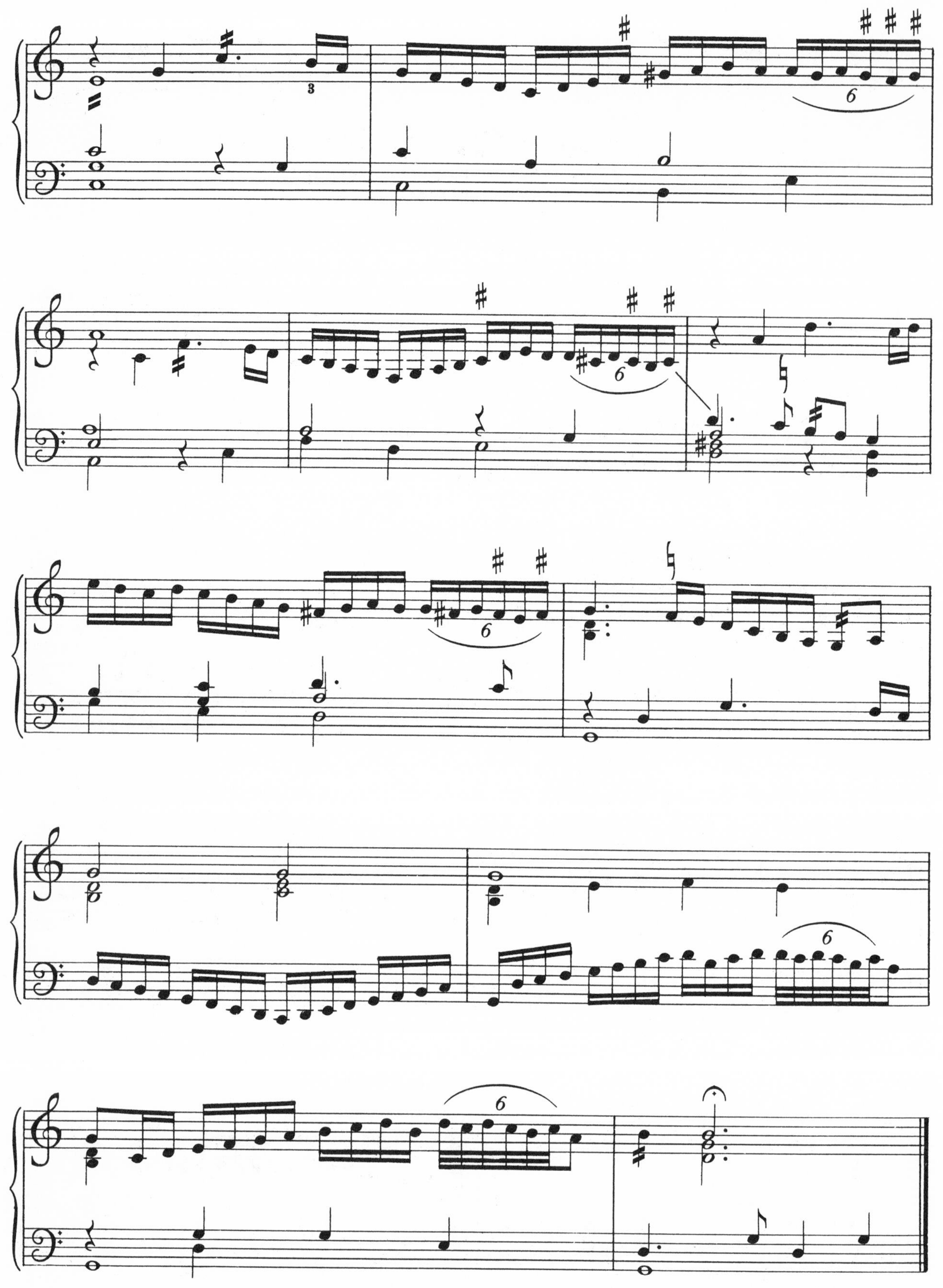
3
6
6
6
6
6
6
finis: mr.w.birde.

13. THE GALLIARDE TO THE SECONDE PAVIAN.

1) E instead of D in MS.

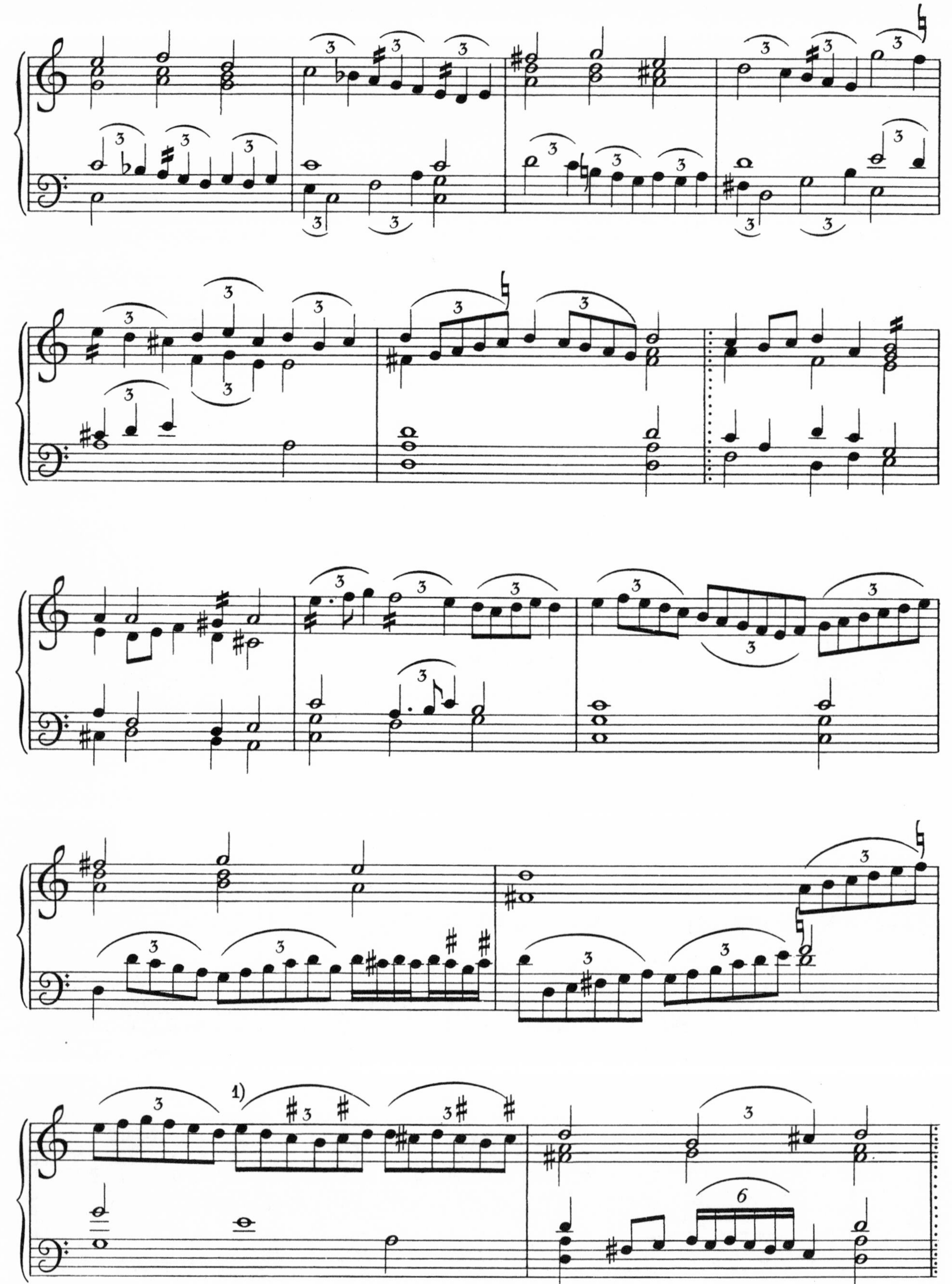

1) two extra quavers, C and D interpolated here in MS. This reading from Add. 30485.

6
finis. mr. w. birde.

14. THE THIRD PAVIAN.

1) barline here in MS.

1) C a dotted minim in MS.   2) G a dotted crotchet in MS.

1) quavers in MS.

mr. w. birde.

15. THE GALLIARDE TO THE THIRD PAVIAN.

1) barline here in MS.

mr. w. birde.

16. THE FOURTH PAVIAN.

1) E not dotted in MS.
2) a crotchet rest in MS. followed by a quaver G and six semiquavers.

1) dotted crotchet in MS. 2) crotchet in MS.

1) semiquaver in MS.

mr. w. birde. the galliarde heere foloweth

17. THE GALLIARDE TO THE FOURTH PAVIAN.

1) barline here in MS.

1) G# in MS.

mr. w. birde. homo memorabilis.

18. THE FIFTE PAVIAN.

1) dotted minim in MS.

1) semiquavers in MS.

1) semiquavers in MS.

19. THE GALLIARDE TO THE FIFTE PAVIAN.

mr. w. birde, laudes deo.

20. PAVANA THE SIXTE: KINBRUGH GOODD.

1) a minim rest here in MS.

1) E only indicated by direct in MS.

1) quaver in MS. 2) B instead of C in MS.

mr. w. birde. the galliarde folows.

21. THE GALLIARDE TO THE SIXTE PAVIAN.

1) minim in MS. 2) not dotted in MS.

laus sit deo. mr. w. birde.

22. THE SEVENTH PAVIAN.

1) D omitted in MS. c.f. bar 8, p. 118. 2) A♯ in MS. instead of F♯. The cannon is slightly altered from the corresponding passage in the section immediately before; c.f. C♮ and F♮ in bars 8 and 9, p. 118. 3) A a minim in MS.

mr. w. birde. gentleman of the chappell.

23. THE EIGHTE PAVIAN.

6

6
5

mr. w. birde. of the chappell.

24 THE PASSINGE MESURES: THE NYNTHE PAVIAN.

1) quavers in MS.

1) semibreve in MS. 2) tenor part, A & B, is omitted in MS.; supplied from Add. 30486. 3) crotchet rest in MS.

1) double barline here in MS. 2) quavers in MS. 3) B is a semiquaver in MS., making the bar incomplete; the quaver is supplied from Add 30486.

1) F♯ in MS.

1) D a quaver in MS.; crotchet supplied from Add. 30486.

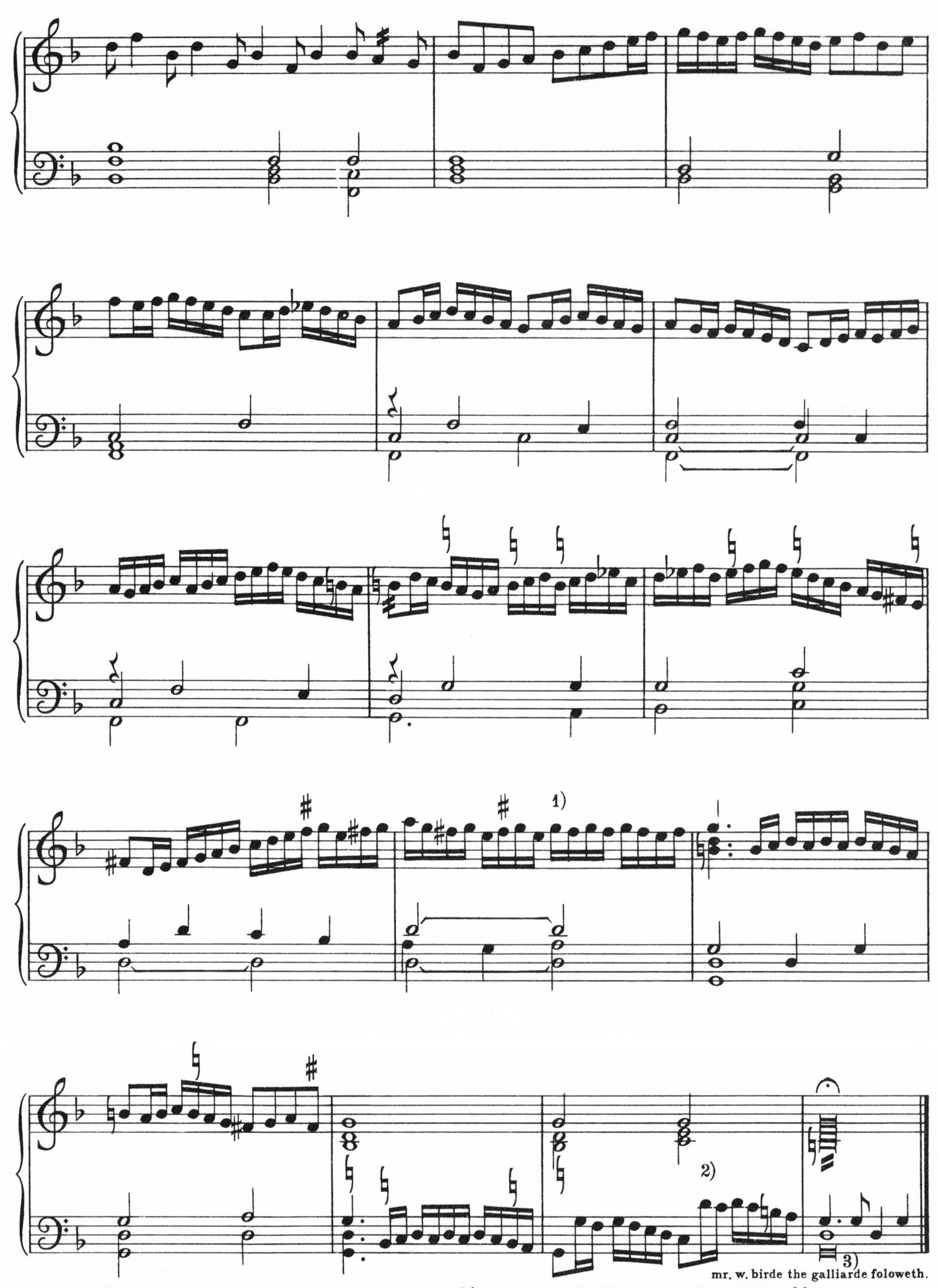

1) the first G of this shake omitted in MS.; corrected from Add. 30486. 2) quavers in MS.; corrected from Add. 30486.

3) F in MS.

25. THE GALLIARDE TO THE NYNTHE PAVIAN.

1) in the MS. there is an E♭ in the signature, intermittent, and left out altogether in the last two sections. It is presumably a copyist's mistake. 2) not dotted in MS. 3) not tied in MS.

1) this entire bar is omitted in MS., making the section one bar short; the missing bar is supplied from Add 30486.
2) A and D instead of B and F in MS.

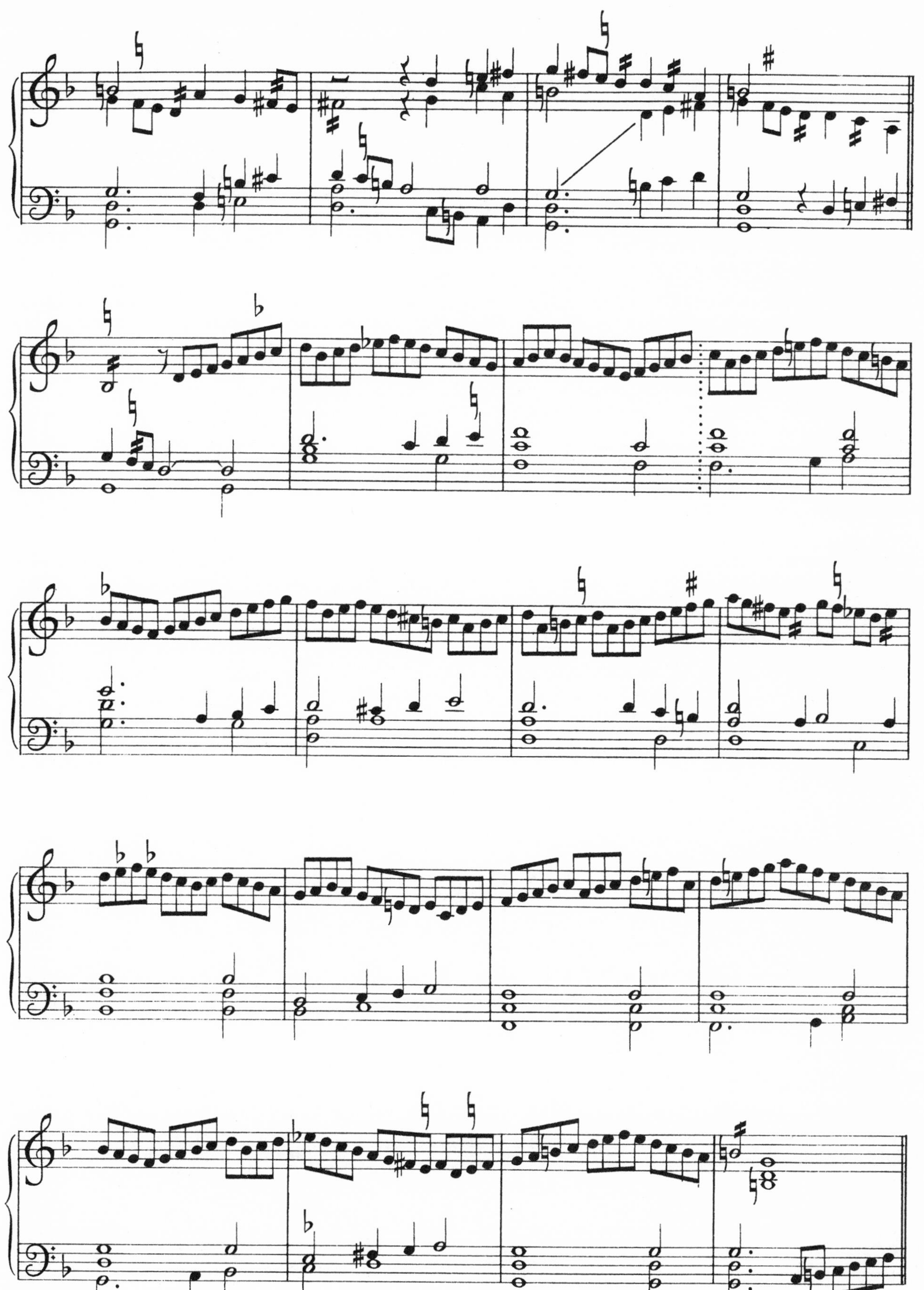

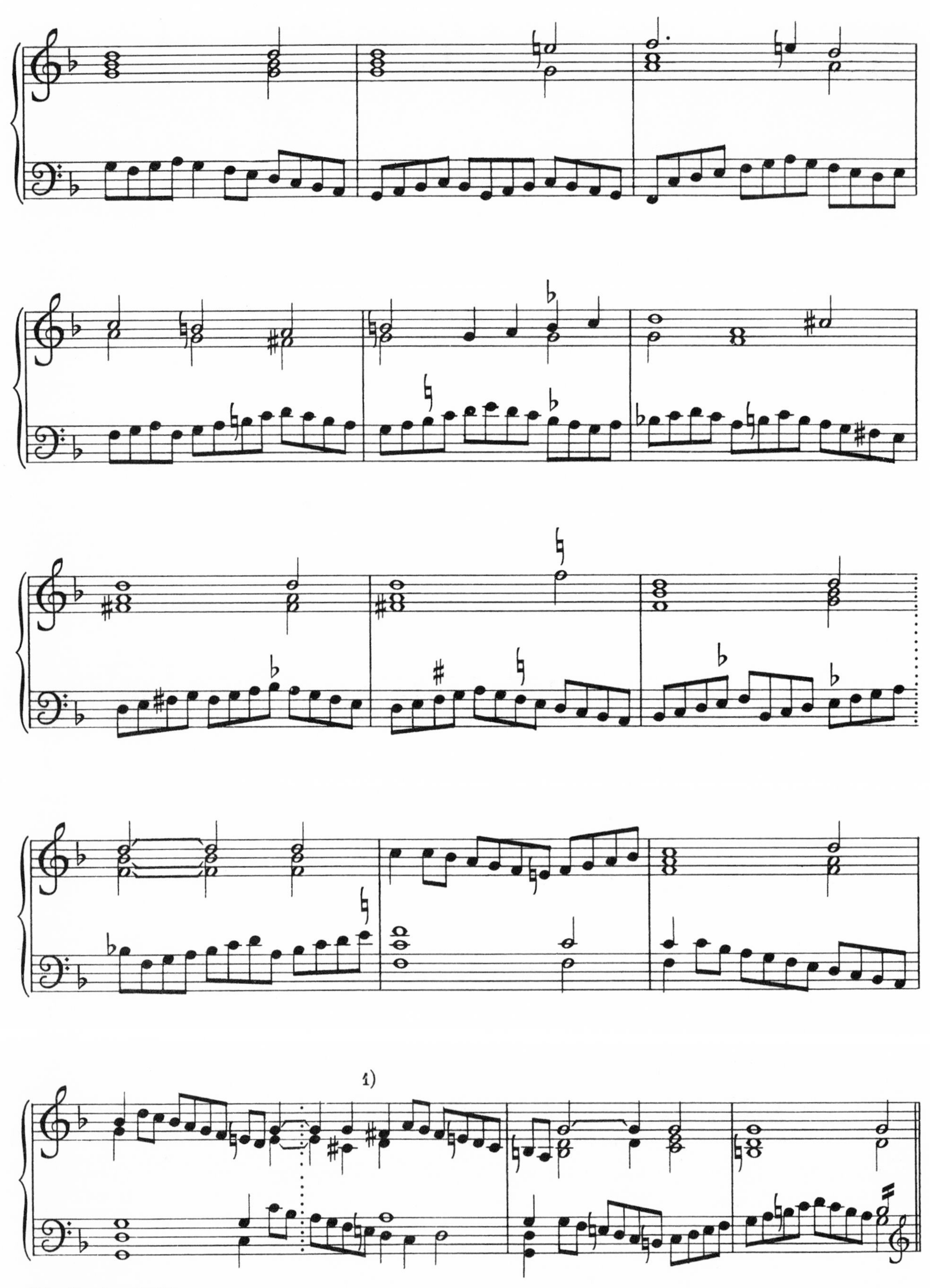

1) barline here in MS.

1) barline here in MS.

1) barline here in MS. 2) D a minim in MS.

mr. w. birde of the chapell.

26. A VOLUNTARIE:

for my ladye nevell.

1) the MS. has A.F.C. instead of A.E.C. here.

finis. mr. w. birde.

1) dotted minim in MS   2) quaver rest in MS. and E in bass a quaver.

27. WILL YOW WALKE THE WOODS SOE WYLDE.

3
5 5 5

1) G not in MS.;supplied from Fitzwilliam reading.

finis mr. w. birde anno dñi 1590.

28. THE MAIDENS SONGE.

1) E instead of D in MS.

1) G not tied in MS.

1) D in MS. instead of C.

6
6
3

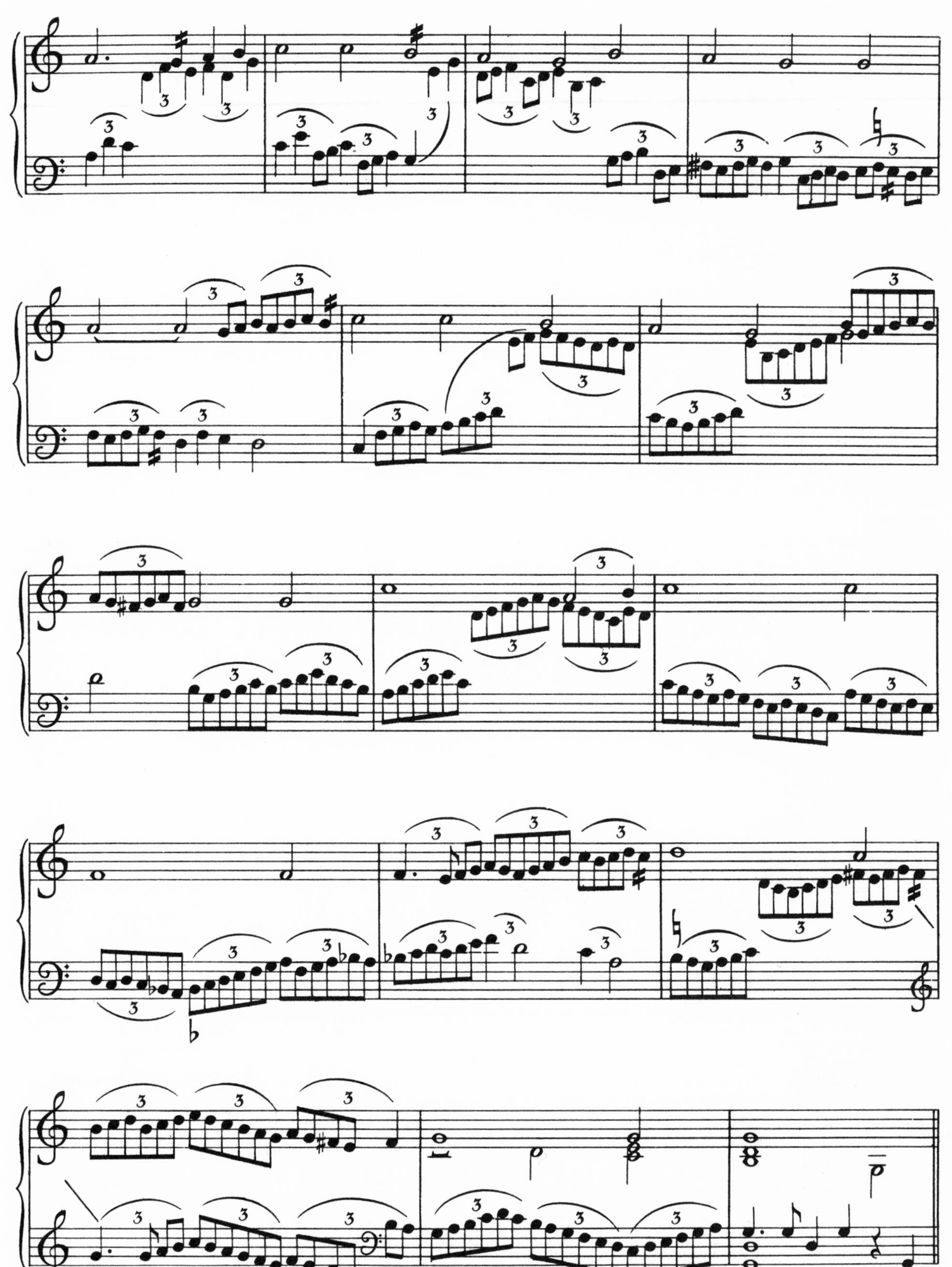

mr. w. birde.

29. A LESSON OF VOLUNTARIE.

1) semibreve A in MS.

1) B and A only indicated by direct in MS.

finis: mr. w birde.

30. THE SECOND GROWNDE.

1) two semiquavers, C and B, omitted in MS.

1) C only indicated in MS. by the sharp. 2) F# in MS.

1) double barline here in MS.

1) B instead of A in MS.

1) B instead of A in MS.

1) A semibreve not in MS.

2) the alto part in this bar is a third lower in MS.

1) the last two quavers, D and E, are omitted in MS.; the barline is one beat earlier. 2) minim in MS. 3) E a dotted minim in MS.

13
14

1) crotchet rest here in MS.

1) G a quaver in MS.

mr.w. birde.

31. HAVE WITH YOW TO WALSINGAME.

1) G a crotchet in MS.   2) E a quaver in MS.

1) barline here in MS. 2) quaver in MS.

1) C♯ in MS.

13
14
15

1) C♯ in MS. obviously for B♮.

1) G instead of F in MS.

1) B a dotted quaver in MS.

finis: maister w. birde.

32. ALL IN A GARDEN GRINE.

1) barline here in MS. 2) A instead of G in MS. 3) a quaver rest here in MS. and the last note A a quaver.

4
F♮
6
6
6
6
6
F♮
6
6♯

1) C♯ in MS. 2) this bar is omitted in its proper place in the MS. (on f. 145) and there is a footnote:— "here is a falte, a pointe left out, wh ye shall finde prickte after the end of the next songe upon the 148 leafe:" and at the bottom of f. 148 the missing bar is written with the note: "this pointe bee longeth to the song before 145 leafe".

1) this chord is a third lower in MS.

mr. w. bird.

33. LORD WILLOBIES WELCOME HOME.

1) A not in MS. 2) G♯ in MS.

1) a quaver in MS., and the barline one quaver later.

1) C♯ in MS. 2) this chord is a fifth higher in MS., F♯. A.D.

finis. maister. willm̃. birde.

34. THE CARMANS WHISTLE.

2
3
5

4
5
5
5
5
4
5
3

finis. maister willm̃. birde.

35. HUGHE ASHTONS GROWNDE.

1) semibreve in MS.

3
4
C♮

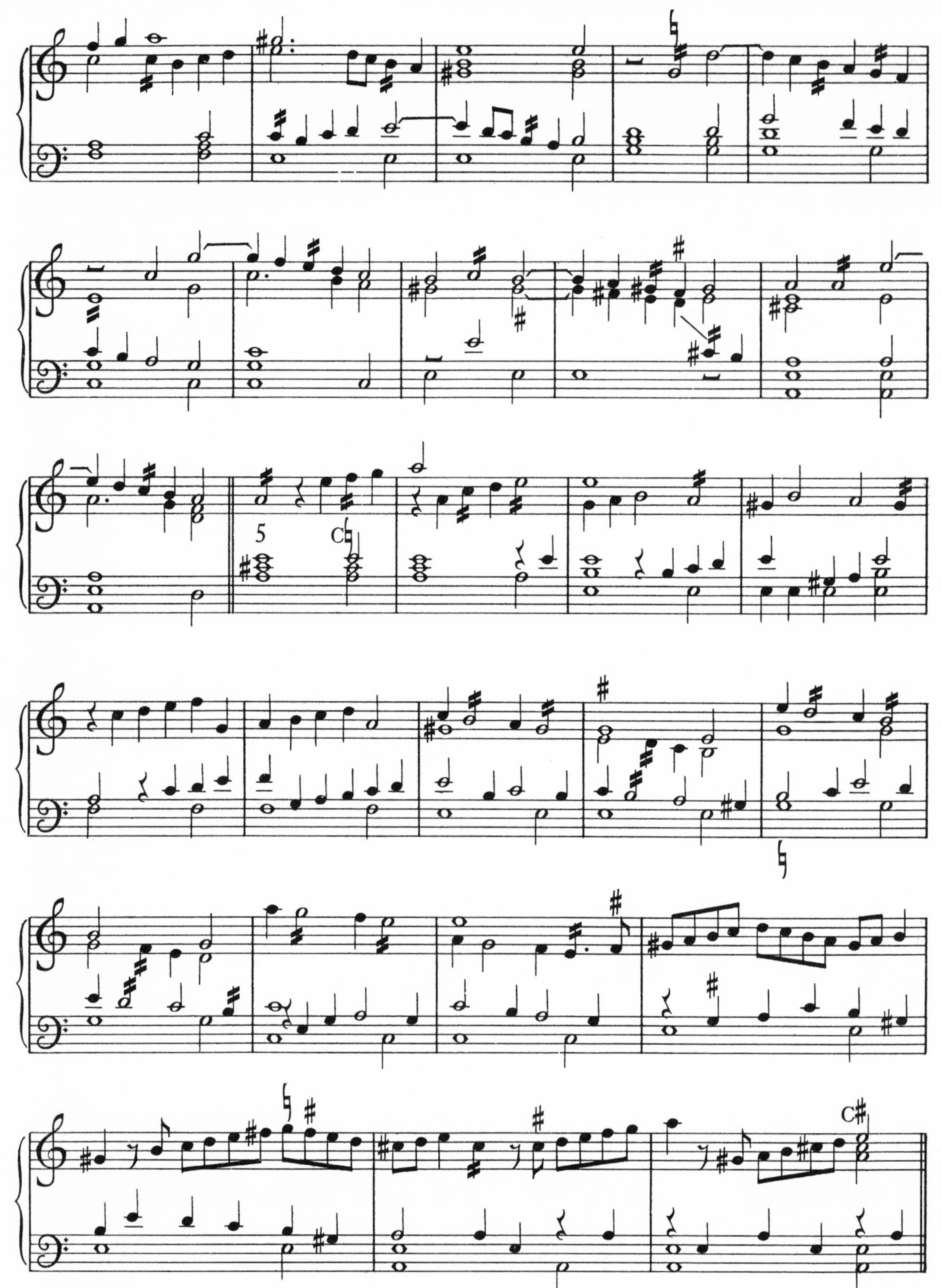
5
C♮
C♯

1) G♯ instead of F♯ in MS.

7
8

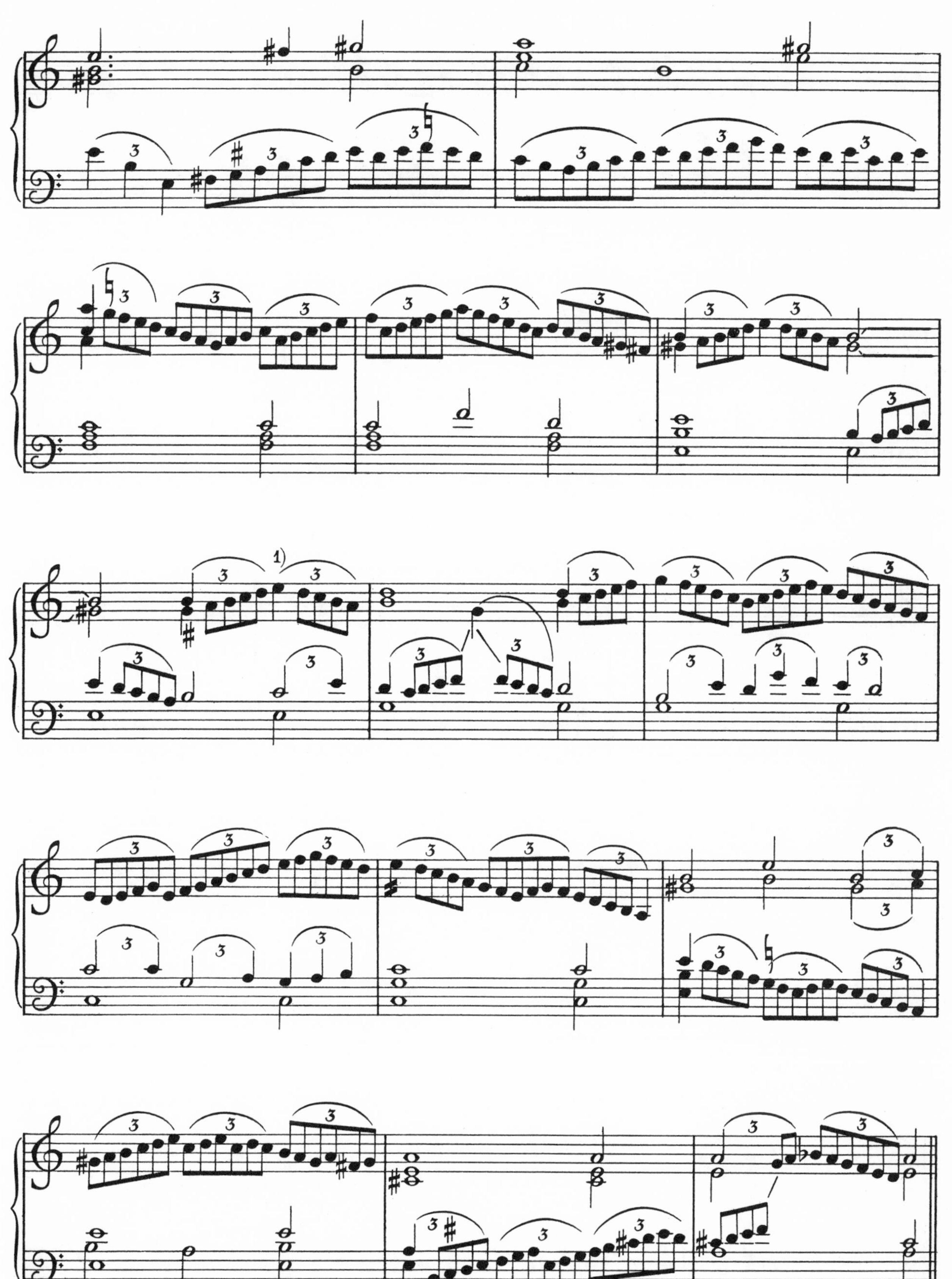

1) E a quaver in MS. and the final quaver A omitted.

1) E instead of G indicated in MS. by direct.

1) an extra barline here in MS.

mr. w. birde

36. A FANCIE.

1) E♮ for F♯ in MS. 2) F♯ in MS.

1) F a semibreve in MS.

5
5
5
5
6
2
2

1) A & C in MS. instead of F & A.

mr. w. birde

37. SELLINGERS ROWNDE.

1) no signature in MS.

1) minim in MS., not tied crotchets

3

1 there is here an extra bar in the MS. which if left makes the tune one bar too long.

1) crotchet rest here in MS. 2) minim in MS. not tied crotchets.

6

1) D in MS. instead of E. 2) minim in MS. not tied crotchets.

1) minim in MS. not tied crotchets. 2) this variation is wrongly numbered to begin five bars earlier.
3) this bar is one crotchet short in the MS.–D & B are omitted. 4) minim in MS.

1) minim in MS., not tied crotchets.

finis. mr. willm̃. birde.

1) quaver in MS.

38. MUNSERS ALMAINE.

1) no signature in MS. 2) not tied in MS.

1) quaver in MS.

1) quaver in MS.

1) quaver rest in MS. 2) quaver in MS. 3) dotted minims in MS.

1) B a quaver in MS. 2) C in MS. instead of D. 3) G not in MS.

1) A♯ in MS. 2) G not in MS.; supplied from Forster reading.

finis. mr. w. birde.

39. THE TENNTHE PAVIAN: MR. W. PETER.

1
2
2
2

1) A quaver in MS 2) semiquaver in MS.; corrected in Drexel and Add. 30486.

1) this E has a flat and a natural in MS.

1) last three semiquavers repeated in MS.

40. THE GALLIARDE TO THE TENNTHE PAVIAN.

1) G a minim in MS.

1) extra barline here in MS.

1) in the MS. the bar ends at A: this reading supplied from Forster.
2) quaver rest here in MS. 3) quavers in MS. 4) quaver rest in MS.

finis mr. w. birde.

41. A FANCIE.

1) there is a minim rest before D in MS. 2) barline here in MS.

1) barline here in MS

1) barline here in MS.

1) E instead of D in MS

1) this obviously correct reading is supplied from Add. 30485. In the MS. the whole passage is a third higher, and the first D&E omitted, making the bar two semiquavers short. 2) semiquaver in MS. 3) G omitted in MS.; supplied from Add. 30485.

42. A VOLUNTARIE.

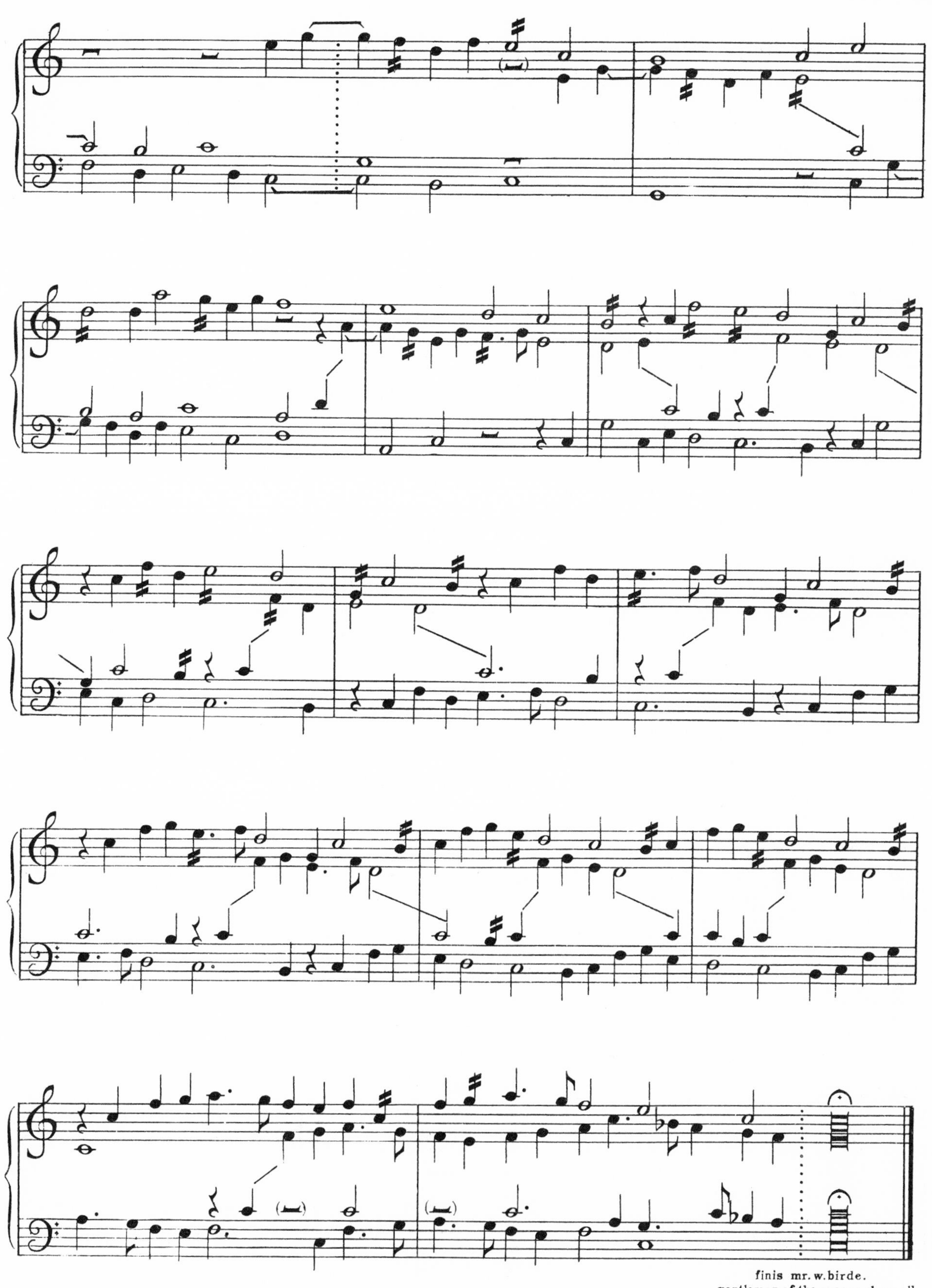

finis mr. w. birde.
gentleman of the queens chappell.